"If you want to learn something new, all you have to do is study something that was written 100 years ago."

— Jeffrey Gitomer

# *Jeffrey Gitomer's*
# LITTLE PLATINUM BOOK
## OF
# CHA-CHING!

*+≡ 32.5 Strategies ≡+*
*To Ring Your Own*
*(Cash) Register of Business*
*And Personal Success*

**FT** Press
FINANCIAL TIMES

**The Little Platinum Book of Cha-Ching!**

© 2007 Pearson Education, Inc. Publishing as FT Press
Upper Saddle River, New Jersey 07458
Vice President and Editor-in-Chief: Tim Moore

To order additional copies of this title, contact your local bookseller or call 704/333-1112.

The author may be contacted at the following address:
Buy Gitomer
310 Arlington Ave, Loft 329
Charlotte, NC 28203
Phone: 704/333-1112 Fax: 704/333-1011
E-mail: salesman@gitomer.com
Web sites: www.gitomer.com, www.trainone.com

Content and style editor: Jessica McDougall
Page designer: Mike Wolff
Cover designer: Josh Gitomer
Cover illustration: Dave Pinski

Printed in China by RR Donnelley.

First Printing, September 2007

Library of Congress Cataloging-in-Publication Data available upon request.

Gitomer, Jeffrey H.
   Little platinum book of cha-ching! : 17.5 strategies to ring your own (cash) register in business and personal success / Jeffrey Gitomer.
      p. cm.
   ISBN 0-13-236274-0 (hardback : alk. paper)
   ISBN 978-0-13-236274-0
   1. Success in business. 2. Selling. 3. Self-actualization (Psychology)
4. Patterson, John Henry, 1844-1922. I. Title.
   HF5386.G487 2008
   650.1--dc22

                                                    2007027807

## THE PATTERSON PRINCIPLES OF SELLING

has been expanded and revised to become

*Jeffrey Gitomer's*
LITTLE PLATINUM BOOK
*of* CHA-CHING!

When I wrote *The Patterson Principles of Selling* in 1998, I took one tenth of the depth of John Patterson and clarified it for salespeople. Everyone who read it loved it.

But John Patterson was not just a sales genius – he was a BUSINESS genius.

I have taken a great sales book and added and expanded on the aspect of business success. And rather than calling them the Patterson/Gitomer Principles, they're referred to throughout this book as **The Cha-Ching! Principles of Business Success**. Each of them plays its own integral role in your business. Each principle is like an instrument in an orchestra. It can stand alone, but it's better, and more powerful, when played together.

And, like any symphony or musical piece, each one of these Cha-Ching! Principles has to be practiced until mastered and has to be played in harmony with the other.

**NOTE:** In every symphony, there's a conductor. That would be you. Your job is not just leading the orchestra, but conducting yourself as a businessperson, and implementing these principles in your own style, in your own manner, and in your own way – with passion, and to the BEST of your ability. When you do, you'll find success and fulfillment.

You hold in your hands the *upgraded, added to, expanded,* and *in-depth* version of business wisdom of 100 years ago from a man who fathered the American Industrial Revolution and founded principles of success, personal development, and sales.

These are principles that you can use and profit from.

If you're looking to grow and succeed in your business career, your entrepreneurial venture, or your sales career, this is your golden opportunity to learn from masters, maybe *the* masters. All the Cha-Ching! Principles have been translated (by me) to today's world and today's business environment. Your environment.

You hold in your hands the opportunity to **RING YOUR OWN REGISTER** and **KEEP THE CASH!**

# Picture your business in 1880

No computer.
No e-mail.
No fax.
No paved roads. (No need – there were no cars.)
No TV.
No radio.
No copy machine.

Heat was provided by coal, and there was no air conditioning. *Sound inviting so far?*

If you wanted to get somewhere, you took a train. If you wanted to connect with someone quickly, you sent a telegram. Otherwise, you sent a letter – handwritten, as there were no typewriters. The light bulb (Edison) was one year old and the telephone was four years old, but there was no system for calling anyone yet.

In 1880, there wasn't much of anything as we know it today.

But it was the year John Patterson bought the patent for an invention called "the cash register" from James Ritty and formed The National Cash Register Company (NCR) in Dayton, Ohio.

Because of Patterson's business methods and strategies, The National Cash Register Company not only became successful, it also attracted successful people.

People like Thomas Watson, who went on to found International Business Machines (you know it now as IBM), and Charles Kettering, who went on to found Dayton Engineering Laboratories Company (DELCO), invented the electric ignition system, sold his company to General Motors, and is recognized as the father of their success.

Dayton was a hotbed of talent. People like The Wright Brothers had their bicycle manufacturing business there.

John Patterson was a thinker, a reader, a strategist, a trainer, a salesman, and a leader of men and women. Patterson was a disciplinarian and a progressive thinker.

**KEEP IN MIND:** There were no business models to build on or study. There was no TQM, Six Sigma, SCORM, or *Good to Great.*

Patterson and the other industrialists like Andrew Carnegie and Andrew Mellon were the ones who *created* the models.

## They didn't follow the leaders.
## They *were* the leaders.

It was the true beginning of the American Business and Industrial Revolution.

About now you're probably thinking: **SO WHAT?**

**HERE'S WHAT:** Over time, many of the success principles that won in the revolution got lost as ad agencies, marketing departments, short-term thinkers, Wall Streeters, and greed barons slowly took over. (Who and what are greed barons? Just take a look at the jails; they're filling up with them – they're also known as corporate executives.)

**LOST AND FOUND:** I'm about to share the lost principles that not only founded the industrial revolution; they are also the principles that created fortunes. Not just money – real wealth.

These principles are easy to understand and easy to apply. There's no rocket science, no mathematical formulas, no graphs, and very few charts.

**GOOD NEWS:** You can adapt these Cha-Ching! Principles with ease and convert them to your success, your wealth, and your fulfillment.

**REAL NEWS:** These are principles that I use and have used to create my success, my wealth, and my fulfillment. I have modified them by adding my thoughts, philosophies, and strategies to bring them into the 21st century. And I have added a few principles to accommodate the business elements that were missing a hundred years ago.

As you read these principles, adapt and apply them to your own business and career to create your own Cha-Ching!

I have a long-sleeved t-shirt that says "You may think I'm a dreamer" on the front of it. I often wear it when I'm working. Especially at night. It's soft and warm. But it's also reality.

# In order to turn your dreams into success, you gotta work. You gotta work hard, you gotta work consistently, and you gotta work continually to improve and ultimately be your best.

You can dream all you want. But at some point, the dream will fade unless the hard work begins to create the results.

Cha-Ching! is a metaphor for success. You may know it as the sound of a cash register ringing – but throughout this book Cha-Ching! will be referred to in every aspect of business. It's about hiring the right people, creating the best principles, teaching and training, encouragement, making a deal, the courage to grow, and every other aspect of business as relates to success and money.

If you own *The Patterson Principles of Selling*, you'll note that there are tremendous similarities in both books. There's a reason. The basis for business success is sales success – but the selling part of the process is only one aspect of the business process. There's also the people, the product, the strategies, the morale, the leadership, and all the other aspects of a business that make selling possible. Cha-Ching! will reveal these in a way that you will be able to understand, apply, become proficient at, and ultimately master the principles that can make your business great.

There a combination of early master's principles like John Patterson, strategies that have made business successful, my ability to interpret those principles and modify them to modern times, and creating a relatable, real-world aspect to each one so that you can implement them almost the minute you read them.

My objective in creating this book is for you to capture the value and the lessons from how other people have rung their register so that you can ring yours. And I thank you for buying this book and helping me ring mine.

# "Everyone has 'the dream.' To make your dream a reality you need the plan, the process, the people, the persistence, the patience, and the passion."

*– Jeffrey Gitomer*

# Do you hear that sound?

Cha-Ching! is a sound familiar to all. It's the sound of the cash register ringing.

Patterson's role in creating success principles fits perfectly because his vehicle and his metaphor were the cash register. Every time it rang, he made money – one transaction at a time, one relationship at a time, one sale at a time, one success at a time, one day at a time.

**Cha-Ching! is the sound of a cash register ringing up a sale.** It registers the amount and says "Thank You" when you print the receipt. *How are you ringing your register?*

**Cha-Ching! is the sound of achievement.** It tells you that you have accomplished something. It rewards your hard work. *What is your sound of achievement?*

**Cha-Ching! is the sound of motivation and inspiration.** It's the YES! of making things happen. You ring the register, and you're motivated to ring it again. *What is the sound of your motivation?*

**Cha-Ching! is the sound of success.** The continued achievement, motivation, and inspiration, adding up to a choir of melodic sweetness. It's the sweet sound of success. *What is your sound of success?*

**Cha-Ching! is the sound of money.** The register is ringing, and the coins are singing. The bills are rustling, and the credit cards are clicking. *What is your sound of money?*

**Cha-Ching! is the sound of wealth.** There's an unspoken peacefulness when wealth arrives. Not having to scramble or struggle but still respecting the process that brought you there. A harmony of understanding and respect. *What is your sound of wealth?*

**Cha-Ching! is the sound of fulfillment.** Not just success – happiness. The sound you hear is "Om." All notes collide to form the sound of heaven on earth. *What is your sound of fulfillment?*

**Cha-Ching! is the sound of music.** Music that makes you feel great every time you hear it. Not just rhythm, Cha-Ching! also sets the tone for more Cha-Chings! and gives you the self-confidence that if you have rung the register once, you can ring it again and again (and again).

Whatever your dreams, whatever your desires, whatever your goals, I challenge you to ring your register at every opportunity. That sound, that music, will confirm your hard work, and, at the same time, build your self-confidence and encourage you to greater heights. That's a powerful path to getting what you want – and earning what you deserve. **Cha-Ching!**

# I have done the research, and discovered the original strategies that built a multimillion-dollar empire at the turn of the last century. I've converted them, added to them, and advanced the technology from trains, telegrams, and tents – to computers, Internet, cell phones, and the Ritz Carlton.

*– Jeffrey Gitomer*

*Jeffrey Gitomer's*
# LITTLE PLATINUM BOOK
## OF
# CHA-CHING!

## *Table of Contents*

# How do you succeed?

**THINK!** about what you have learned from your father and mother. Their wisdom has laid the path and built the foundation of your philosophy, your belief system, your personality, and your achievement.

From there, you learned and developed success attributes from others, both alive and dead.

My parents have passed on. Many of my mentors and role models of business – John Patterson (sales and business success), PT Barnum (promotion and public relations), Orison Swett Marden (success and persistence), Dale Carnegie (making friends and public speaking), Napoleon Hill (attitude and goals), Ayn Rand (writing style and philosophy), Earl Nightingale (*The Strangest Secret*), and Groucho Marx (humor) – have all passed on.

But what I learned from them, and continue to learn from them by reading, studying, and applying their wisdom has helped me to the place and position I am in today.

I am successful because I have remained a student. And as I get further up the ladder, I study harder and work harder. "Take it easy" is not in my lexicon. Never will be.

This book is a classic example of what I have learned. I'm passing the condensed version of that wisdom on to you.

# Business and personal success

Everyone wants success.

Very few are willing to work hard to achieve it. Few are willing to study and apply lessons from the masters who have already done it. Even fewer love what they do enough to ring the cash register of sales, business, and life.

*Here are the facts of why – why no and why yes:*

It seems as though people who went into business or took a position for the money, and not the love, didn't get what they wanted. His or her passion for money exceeded their passion for what they were about to do – love of buck, rather than love of what they were doing. And when the money failed to manifest itself, they quit – often quitting what would have been a success if they loved it enough to have stuck it out.

**FACE IT:** No one goes into any job or venture thinking "I'm going to fail at this." Everyone WANTS to succeed. But, still, very few do.

**IF YOU ARE LOOKING TO SUCCEED:** There are elements that you have to plan for, have passion for, and ultimately master in order to grab the brass ring and keep it in your hand.

*And if you look at the story of John Patterson, the elements become much more clear. Here they are...*

- **An idea you believe will work.**

- **Clear vision of what it takes to win.**
  **"A definite major aim," to quote Napoleon Hill.**

- **Seeing the opportunity and grasping it.**

- **The courage to see through the tough times.**

- **The risk tolerance to see obstacles as temporary.**

- **Decisiveness about the day and the issues you face.**

- **Good people to help you.**

- **Knowledge of what you're doing.**
  **And a willingness to learn what's new.**

- **Wisdom from others who have done it.**

- **True desire to succeed beyond money.**

- **Love of whatever it is you're doing.**

Look at these elements, and evaluate yourself against them. How high can you rate yourself?

If you're seeking gold (or platinum), seven on a scale of ten is the minimum rating to gain wealth. Or, better stated, *to ring your register.* If you're going to take the entrepreneurial plunge, if you're going to reach for the business brass ring, the higher you can achieve excellence in each one of these elements, the more likely the ring will be yours.

# Learn to be successful from people who have succeeded

"People don't like to be sold, but they love to buy" is a registered trademark phrase of mine. It's my sales mantra, and I have used it for years.

My research director of *The Patterson Principles of Selling*, Amanda Desrochers, screamed, "Jeffrey! Listen to this! 'If the prospect understood the proposition, he would not have to be sold; he would come to buy.' It's a Patterson quote."

She chortled with delight.
"You guys have the same thoughts!"

I wasn't surprised. But I was amazed (and gratified) at the similarity of our philosophy and the span of time where so much has changed – yet the strategy of effecting the change has remained the same.

One hundred years separated those statements, but, philosophically, they're less than a centimeter apart.

There's an old saying, "The more things change, the more they remain the same." Like many of the greatest thoughts and sayings, it has stood the test of time because it's true.

I got the idea to revive Patterson's principles after presenting to The National Cash Register Company at their annual sales conferences in Miami and Cannes.

As a success and business historian, I'd always known of Patterson, but I had no idea of the depth of his strategies and achievements.

After doing major research at NCR and the Dayton/ Montgomery County Historical Society (that houses all the treasures of NCR), I realized, "This guy is one of the founders of American business success and *the* father of American salesmanship – and his principles are buried."

Patterson's principles are applicable to **ANYONE WANTING TO BE SUCCESSFUL IN BUSINESS**. If that's you, read this book, study this book, apply this book, and get it to everyone in your organization so that they understand your philosophy and are on the same page (literally) of thought and process to discover success.

This book is your opportunity to learn business at the feet of John Patterson, the founder and president of The National Cash Register Company, and the original master salesman and entrepreneur of America.

Keep in mind that these success principles were created before things like the telephone or the automobile existed. Paved roads were not yet the order of the day. It was the beginning of the manufacturing revolution in America. And John Patterson decided to take a leadership position.

After I read and studied, I discovered that Patterson was instrumental in fathering many aspects of the business and industrial revolution.

*Here's a short list:*

**One of the fathers of self-improvement**

**One of the fathers of leadership**

**One of the fathers of business creativity**

**One of the fathers of positive thinking**

**One of the fathers of business systems**

**One of the fathers of business technology**

**One of the fathers of pay incentives and recognition**

**One of the fathers of Fortune 500 companies**

**One of the fathers of success**

**THINK ABOUT THIS:** It was Patterson who coined the word THINK! that everyone credits to Thomas Watson and IBM. What people don't know is that Watson worked for Patterson, took it when he left, and used it to help begin the legend of IBM.

**THINK ABOUT THIS:** It was Patterson who created the original personality sales model. It was Patterson who created the first book on how to deal with sales objections. It was Patterson who held the first sales boot camps. In tents. In fields. Patterson didn't call potential customers prospects or suspects; he referred to them as "probable purchasers."

# John Patterson was the father of...

John Patterson, President of The National Cash Register Company, was a visionary, a thinking, an entrepreneur, a risk-taker, a reader, a teacher, a student, and a salesman. Certainly the best salesman of his time. Arguably the best salesman of all time.

Patterson's success was due to his ability to blend the emotion that makes the sale with the logic that figures out the reasoning behind it. He had the perfect blend of logic and emotion. Forming opinions or justifying decisions leans toward being logical, but Patterson understood that the process of buying was an emotional one.

He knew it. And he taught it.

## Not just a businessman, Patterson was the creator of most of the practices that distinguish modern American business from all other businesses in the world.

Not just a salesman, he was the founder of modern salesmanship. Not just a speaker, he was among the most effective of public demonstrators. Not just a financier, he was the chief exponent of getting money by spending money. Not just a manufacturer, he was the originator of the modern American factory.

Not just a judge or a picker of men, he was the father of organized business and the developer of more business leaders than any other man of his time. Not just a man of commanding personality, he was a rare leader of men – equally sure of himself in threatened defeat as he was in expected victory.

Patterson was a founding father of personal development for business excellence, stressing the similarity between physical readiness, mental readiness, and success. Patterson trained his people the same way he trained himself. With passion and intensity.

But far and away, the overwhelming evidence of his genius was his concept of...

"Creating the demand for a receipt, rather than just trying to sell the concept of a cash register."

*Patterson was salesmanship's father because he...*

- **Was the first person who realized a customer was more likely to complete a transaction through buying than selling.**

- **Created the original "pull through" model.**

- **Pioneered sales training.**

- **Taught his men to adapt and harmonize with the "probable purchaser" (the prospect).**

- **Inspired his people with ideas that worked.**

- **Backed his salespeople with advertising and promotion so that the NCR brand of cash register was by far the machine of choice.**

*Patterson was a founding father of American business because of...*

- **The strategies he created.**

- **The methods he pioneered.**

- **The manner in which he transferred his genius to his team.**

- **And their track record of success to prove it.**

# Where did John Patterson get his concepts and strategies?

He read.

John Patterson regarded a good book as a great mental possession. Only books worthy of being read again and again were to be found in his private library. His books were marked and underlined, cover to cover. Whenever new knowledge appeared, John Patterson underlined it, bookmarked it, studied it, and put it into practice. Many underlined passages in his books show the essence of the message that captured his attention.

Books helped to shape the man and the empire he built. Patterson believed that a good book was not the plaything for the idle hour, but a veritable means for generating power. He read. And he generated power.

Several years ago, I purchased a collection of books from the original John Patterson library. Most of them were on longevity, plus a few biographies.

I was perusing the books to complete this work and decided to look at every book that I owned of Patterson's – and pulled out the title *He Can Who Thinks He Can* by Orison Swett Marden. My blood ran cold. It's a first edition book published in 1908, and I realized that Patterson and I had yet one more thing in common.

**AUTHOR'S PERSONAL NOTE:** The person Napoleon Hill emulated was Orison Swett Marden. He was the original positive-attitude genius of the 20th century. Lately, I've been buying every Marden book I can get my hands on.

I carry the Marden book from Patterson's library with me now and read a page or two a day. I especially read the parts that Patterson underlined. As usual, he found the gems.

QUOTES UNDERLINED BY THE HAND OF
JOHN PATTERSON, TAKEN FROM THE BOOK

# *He Can Who Thinks He Can*

by Orison Swett Marden
Published in 1908

**EVERY CHILD SHOULD BE TAUGHT
TO EXPECT SUCCESS.**

---

**MULTITUDES OF PEOPLE, ENSLAVED BY BAD
PHYSICAL HABITS, ARE UNABLE TO GET THEIR
BEST SELVES INTO THEIR WORK.**

---

**SOME OF THE GREATEST MEN IN HISTORY NEVER
DISCOVERED THEMSELVES UNTIL THEY LOST
EVERYTHING BUT THEIR PLUCK AND GRIT.**

---

**IT IS EASY TO FIND SUCCESSFUL BUSINESSMEN,
BUT NOT SO EASY TO FIND MEN WHO PUT
CHARACTER ABOVE BUSINESS.**

ALMOST ANYBODY CAN RESOLVE TO DO A
GREAT THING; IT IS ONLY THE STRONG,
DETERMINED CHARACTER THAT PUTS THE
RESOLVE INTO EXECUTION.

---

NO SUBSTITUTE HAS EVER YET BEEN
DISCOVERED FOR HONESTY.

---

HAPPINESS IS A CONDITION OF MIND.

---

RESOLVE THAT YOU WILL BE A MAN OF IDEAS,
ALWAYS ON THE LOOKOUT FOR IMPROVEMENT.

---

POWER GRAVITATES TO THE MAN
WHO KNOWS HOW AND WHY.

---

THERE IS NO WORD IN THE ENGLISH LANGUAGE
MORE MISUSED AND ABUSED THAN LUCK.

---

THE BEST EDUCATED PEOPLE ARE THOSE WHO
ARE ALWAYS LEARNING, ALWAYS ABSORBING
KNOWLEDGE FROM EVERY POSSIBLE SOURCE,
AND AT EVERY OPPORTUNITY.

---

A TEST OF THE QUALITY OF THE INDIVIDUAL IS THE
SPIRIT IN WHICH HE DOES HIS WORK.

**Free Git✗Bit**...**Want the complete list of quotes that Patterson underlined in this book and a register of Marden titles?** Go to www.gitomer.com, register if you are a first-time visitor, and enter the word MARDEN in the GitBit box.

# Ring the register

120 years after John Patterson created the demand for a receipt, people all around the world still live by his basic premise of *ringing the register*. If you're in a retail business, you want to ring your cash register. If you're in any other business, you want to make a ton of sales and be successful. And in your life, you want success both monetarily and personally. Ringing the register is a metaphor that you can relate to and identify with. It's not just a sound, it's a feeling.

More interesting is the fact that I almost overlooked this premise, and were it not for a dinner with the great Pat Hazell at Sullivan's in Charlotte, North Carolina, this AHA! would not have been included. I showed Pat the makings of my book as he toured my studio and office lofts and told him a little bit about Patterson.

Pat had just done a series of events in Dayton, Ohio, and as we discussed the book, he asked if there was a chapter in it called "ringing the register." And I just sat there thinking to myself: *Cha-Ching!* There isn't. But there will be.

Ringing the register is *the* most fundamental aspect of a businessperson's process. If you do everything in the business and sales cycle, but fail to ring the register, then as a businessperson or as a salesperson you have failed. The register, and its accompanying receipt (aka the order), is the measure by which business success or failure is determined. Remember? "Nothing happens until a sale is made." Red Motley, 1946.

## AND SO THE GOAL REMAINS THE SAME:

Your company vision may be different. Your company mission may be different. Your company's product may be different. Your company's service may be different. The way you do business may be different.

But you all have the same goal. Ring the register. Make a connection. Make a sale. Make a deal. Make it happen. Make a success.

And make a fortune.

The NCR Archive at the Montgomery Historical Society

The one-millionth cash register sold by NCR. Cha-Ching!

Whatever John Patterson did or did not do, whatever John Patterson was as a person or was not as a person, whatever John Patterson's intention or vision was or was not, 120 years later the processes that he created and inspired others to create – his incredible leadership actions and principles still cast a shadow and are still at the core of any business's success and every person's success in business.

*You can fly:*

> **Every time a register rings, a business gets its wings.**
>
> **Every time a register rings, a CEO gets his wings.**
>
> **Every time a register rings, an accounting department gets its wings.**
>
> **Every time a register rings, production and inventory get their wings.**
>
> **Every time a register rings, a salesperson gets his or her wings.**

Wanna fly? Ring *your* register!

**HERE'S YOUR CHALLENGE:** Begin with principle one. THINK! And day by day, principle by principle – master each of these strategies and calls to action.

And toward your success, and toward your fulfillment, understand that the goal will always remain: Ring the register, baby. Ring the register.

# Cha-Ching!

Most people are looking for some secret formula for success – you already have the secret within you – this book is written to help you discover it, and take the right actions to cash in.

– *Jeffrey Gitomer*

# The evolution and power of the receipt

Never forget the genius associated with the philosophy: Patterson did not sell the cash register; rather, he created the need and the demand for a receipt.

This may be the most powerful business strategy of the 19th, 20th, *and* 21st century.

Take a minute to ponder how you might use that philosophy to build your business.

- **What demands are you creating?**
- **Who needs what you offer?**
- **Who is calling you to buy?**

Add to this incredible reality that the receipt is one of the most powerful pieces of paper in the world. Every receipt has its own power. It's your PROOF of purchase and ownership. And EVERY purchase is now accompanied by one. Thanks to John Patterson.

Receipts not only prove you bought it, but they prove you own it, can return it, can exchange it, can get a warranty enforced, can resell it, can get reimbursed for it, and can deduct it from your taxes. In many cases, you need to show your receipt to exit a store 30 seconds after you just made the purchase.

You save receipts for years.
They often outlive the very product you bought.

# Get a Receipt

*The NCR Archive at the Montgomery Historical Society*

**NCR promotional photo used in the early 1900s.**

Think of how often you use your receipts. They are documents, they are the reminders marking the passage of your time and your money. Receipts are the one constant in business for the last 100 years. Would you like your receipt in the bag?

The receipt is the only thing in business that has remained intact. A receipt is the "prize" because, without it, you have lost.

Banking and checking accounts give receipts for transactions. Your cancelled check or credit card statement is your receipt. A receipt is not just a proof of purchase – it's a recorded transaction. Proof of payment, with clerk, date, time, etc. It's a valuable document of who did what, when they did it, and how much was involved.

Want your money back? Better have your receipt. IRS knocking at your door? Better have your receipts.

The question, "Do you want a receipt with that?" came way before "Do you want fries with that?"

**"A receipt, like a deed, is proof of title to property."**
*1912 quote from a National Cash Register brochure.*

**"Try to get a refund without one."**
*Jeffrey Gitomer*

# The Probable Purchaser

Patterson's selling philosophy was centered around the concept of referring to a prospect as a probable purchaser, thus defining the prospect and your attitude toward him or her in the *same* breath!

So powerful. It's the biggest sales AHA! I've had since I earned my first commission back in 1963 (yeah, 1963).

To me, probable purchaser is as powerful a philosophy as I have *ever* seen or read. It's well over a hundred years old, AND NO ONE USES IT.

Patterson could have used words like prospect, possible, prospective, and potential. But in his positive attitude thought process, he not only assumed the sale – he put word-thoughts into the minds of his people so they would constantly reinforce their own belief system. Cha-Ching!

Probable purchaser is a classic "lost element" of the Patterson Principles that will not only be resurrected here but that you can also employ every day as you seek success.

# The evolution of
# *The Primer*

John Patterson didn't just believe in the power of training, he lived the essence of it. He realized early on that training was the link to infinite sales and business success. Patterson created the first system of selling.

He selected steps that had won in the past and trained everyone to use them. In your business there are steps that work. Your job is to uncover them, document them, make them the best they can be, re-prove them in the field yourself, and then train them.

The original NCR sales script, "How I Sell A National Cash Register," which became known as *The Primer*, contained instruction on what salesman should say during the sale and what they were to do while saying it. The first *Primer* was introduced in June of 1887.

*The Primer covered the factors that were common to every sale, and divided the sales into four parts:*

1. **The approach to the probable purchaser.**

2. **The demonstration of the register.**

3. **How to overcome objections.**

4. **How to close the sale.**

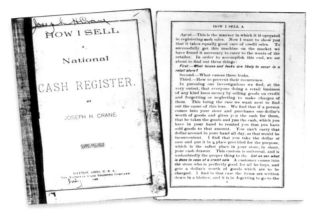

**1887 edition**

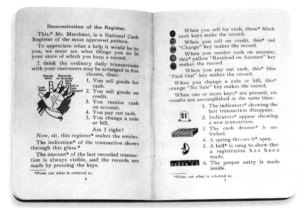

**1923 edition**

"We progress through change."

— *Patterson's favorite quote*

*The Primer* began when Joe Crane, John Patterson's brother-in-law and NCR's best salesman, was asked to sit in on a meeting devoted to the discussion of prices. At the end of the meeting, Crane stated that the price was all right and the product was good, but the salesmen didn't know how to sell it. Crane saw that they were selling in the purchaser's environment. That was where the problem started because they were more susceptible to distractions. Sales distractions. It was much better to take the purchaser elsewhere.

This idea worked phenomenally for Crane, and Patterson wanted his salesmen to follow Crane's lead. Crane said the same thing, word for word, during each demonstration to his probable purchasers.

At first, Patterson thought this would become monotonous and tiresome, but Crane insisted that, "It has never got monotonous yet. The reason it is not monotonous is because it is to different people every time." Crane presented Patterson with one of his demonstrations, after which Patterson stated, "I will call the stenographer; you can dictate this to him and get it typewritten."

When I first read *The Primer* in the Montgomery County Historical Society where the Patterson archives are preserved, it was like I was reading the Holy Grail or the Talmud.

*The Primer* ended with a lesson on the value and importance of keeping physically fit and a chart detailing the "50 ways I can improve myself." Patterson did not think in terms of profit, like most salesmen. Instead, he thought in terms of the good the cash register would bring to the probable purchaser.

He felt that if his salesman could not sell his product, there must be something wrong with the salesman, not the product.

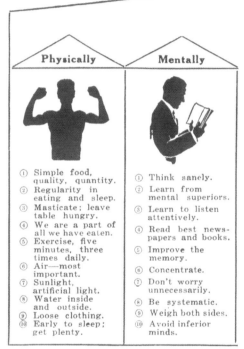

**Physically**

① Simple food, quality, quantity.
② Regularity in eating and sleep.
③ Masticate; leave table hungry.
④ We are a part of all we have eaten.
⑤ Exercise, five minutes, three times daily.
⑥ Air—most important.
⑦ Sunlight, artificial light.
⑧ Water inside and outside.
⑨ Loose clothing.
⑩ Early to sleep; get plenty.

**Mentally**

① Think sanely.
② Learn from mental superiors.
③ Learn to listen attentively.
④ Read best newspapers and books.
⑤ Improve the memory.
⑥ Concentrate.
⑦ Don't worry unnecessarily.
⑧ Be systematic.
⑨ Weigh both sides.
⑩ Avoid inferior minds.

To him, personal appearance was everything. He insisted all his men be clean-shaven, dressed sharp, shoes polished, and healthy, active, awake, and prosperous. If his men followed these 50 ways, they would be on the road to personal and professional success.

The same goes for you — even if you're a woman.

# 50 Ways I Can Improve Myself

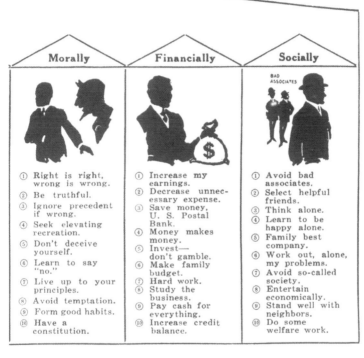

**Morally**

① Right is right, wrong is wrong.
② Be truthful.
③ Ignore precedent if wrong.
④ Seek elevating recreation.
⑤ Don't deceive yourself.
⑥ Learn to say "no."
⑦ Live up to your principles.
⑧ Avoid temptation.
⑨ Form good habits.
⑩ Have a constitution.

**Financially**

① Increase my earnings.
② Decrease unnecessary expense.
③ Save money. U. S. Postal Bank.
④ Money makes money.
⑤ Invest— don't gamble.
⑥ Make family budget.
⑦ Hard work.
⑧ Study the business.
⑨ Pay cash for everything.
⑩ Increase credit balance.

**Socially**

BAD ASSOCIATES

① Avoid bad associates.
② Select helpful friends.
③ Think alone.
④ Learn to be happy alone.
⑤ Family best company.
⑥ Work out, alone, my problems.
⑦ Avoid so-called society.
⑧ Entertain economically.
⑨ Stand well with neighbors.
⑩ Do some welfare work.

The graphic on the right is a "morph" of two of the
classic Patterson images from *The Primer*.
It's telling you what exercise you need to do to be
both physically AND mentally ready to succeed.

# Principles are driven by truth

I have chosen to call these business philosophies and strategies "principles" because they are truths, and it is up to you to implement them into your business and your life.

I would much rather do business with someone who is principle-driven than money-driven. Money-driven people have a few bucks but focus on the money aspect of the transaction rather than the customer aspect of the relationship. And you can smell those people like bad milk.

A principle-driven person has wealth. And that wealth is not just in money. It's in reputation, in the actions that they take, and in their personal pride. And not just their success, but also their fulfillment. A person who lives by their principles is much more likely to be fulfilled when they're counting their money. Everyone counts their money. The real question is *how do you feel when you know the sum-total*. Get it?

Being a person of principle means that you are self-guided. And in that self-guiding way, you will come to inspire yourself and achieve by your own inspiration.

# These principles are more than 100 years old. They have a history of success. All of them are easily understood. None of them break any of your company's rules. Each of them can be mastered with some hard work. Together these principles encompass an approach to the business and sales process that will lead you to success this day, this month, this year, and this lifetime.

*— Jeffrey Gitomer*

# What is a Cha-Ching! Principle, you ask?

A principle is a concept, a strategy, or a thought – that when understood, practiced, and implemented into your business process it becomes part of your philosophy, rather than simply a technique. Principles are the highest form of action and self-belief. "Give me liberty or give me death!" is a principle.

I have uncovered 32 major business principles of John Patterson and I believe they capture the essence of what he preached and practiced. I have added my 21st-century adaptations and concepts so that you can implement these strategies into your quest for success. Many of them spill over from sales, to business, to life. All the better. All the more powerful. All the more valuable to you, whatever your job title or profession.

I have taken the liberty to adjust a word here and there without violating the Patterson way of thinking. Our philosophies are so similar, it's scary. And I have added one of my own. It's the .5 in the 32.5 principles. It's the one that glues the others together. But the real question you're asking right now is:

## "Hey Gitomer, what's in this for me?"

# Here's what you will find as you read each Cha-Ching! Principle...

**QUOTES:** One from Patterson. One from me. And an occasional one from someone else relevant. The quotes emphasize the principle and get you into the groove to think about it. Everyone loves a short burst of information. And the quotes will help clarify what you're about to read and set your mind on the thoughts inside the principle.

**THE DESCRIPTION AND EXPLANATION OF THE PRINCIPLE:**
Each principle is about one element of business as relates to its growth and success. The principles are designed to create an understanding and an awareness and challenge you to think about them as they relate to you and your business and further challenge you to take an action so that you can achieve success, principle by principle – not just at the end of the book.

 **THINK!...AND DO:** The real-world application process to make you THINK. The word THINK! will challenge you to do just that. There will be "thinks" to think about and questions to ask yourself. The THINK! and exercise icon challenges are there to help you understand how to think about the principle. Specifically, how to apply and adapt the concept to your career and your life.

**@BAT. BUSINESS ACTION TRIGGER and BUSINESS ACHIEVEMENT TRIGGER. YOUR OPPORTUNITY TO SWING THE BAT.** People in business and entrepreneurs are like ball players – actually playing the game. They're in the ballpark of business. They have their uniform on and they're standing at the plate with the an opportunity to hit. As a batter, you have an opportunity. The people watching you in the stadium, the spectators (also known as your customers), are either cheering for you or booing you. You've Cha-Chinged them by selling them a ticket and a hot dog. Now is your opportunity to get on base. If you can get a hit one out of three times for 20 years, you'll go to the hall of fame as one of the best who ever played the game. You'll hit your share of home runs and you'll hit your share of doubles. But the object is *make contact, get on base, score a run, win the game.* The **@BAT** icon will appear throughout this book as a business achievement trigger or a business action trigger. It's your opportunity to swing the bat. And score.

The pages that follow are The Cha-Ching! Principles *of* Business Success.

Many of them have been extracted from *The Primer* and other writings by and about John Patterson and the people he employed.

I've added 40 years of entrepreneurial experience, 30 years of sales experience, and 15 years of writing in order for these principles to apply to your business life and business success.

PRINCIPLE 1:

# Think!

**"Think and act – two words of progress."**
*John Patterson*

**"Thinking – an action that very few
people take the time to do."**
*Jeffrey Gitomer*

The word THINK! will carry you through this book. It's
an action that very few people take the time to do – and a
lifetime opportunity to stay ahead and succeed.

Patterson believed that progress was the result of thought.
*What are you thinking about?*

The phrase THINK! was used as a motivational tool for the
workers within Patterson's company. He challenged them
to think about his ideas and principles and he challenged
them to think about how they could take those principles
to the next level. And many did.

A true leader is someone who inspires his people to get
better, not just follow orders. Patterson did both.

In 1911, after NCR's one-millionth register was sold, a
pocket-sized book was printed for the salesmen as a
motivational reminder.

The book was entitled *THINK!* and contained brief passages about what some of the greatest inventors were doing for the world at that time.

"Think of what a great thing Thomas A. Edison did when he thought of the incandescent light" is an example of those passages. At the end of the book, Patterson showed how thought made the cash register a common item in each business for over one million merchants.

*THINK! about taking action on each of these twelve business thoughts every day:*

**How can I uncover new customers?**

**How can I become a better presenter?**

**How does my customer profit from using my product?**

**How did I better myself today?**

**What did I learn new?**

**How can I serve better?**

**Is my attitude better today than it was yesterday?**

**Are my customers loyal today?**

**How am I investing my time today?**

**Did I get a referral today?**

**Did I give a referral today?**

**Did I work on my legacy today?**

*Then try these six personal thoughts:*

**How connected am I with the one I love?**

**What can I do each day to stay better connected and show more love?**

**What am I doing for myself that's making me a better person?**

**What could I (should I) be doing to improve myself and my quality of life?**

**What am I doing to have more laughs and more fun?**

**What am I doing to think deeper and challenge myself each day?**

# Thinking, like any other action, is a discipline.

# You decide your own outcome based on your desire and self-determination.

Realize early on as you read this book that every principle takes thinking on your part to understand it and action on your part to master it. Those "thoughts" will be the backbone of your ideas and their implementation – your actions to succeed.

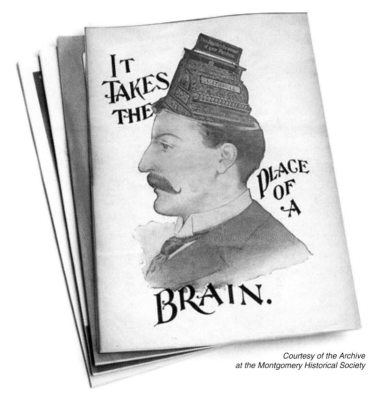

*Courtesy of the Archive
at the Montgomery Historical Society*

This image appeared on the back cover
of the June 1894 issue of *The Hustler*.

Most people have no idea how to spend time in thought. Try writing your thoughts as you come up with them. This way you preserve and clarify your thinking.

**AUTHOR'S NOTE:** I have been writing my thoughts for more than 40 years. It's not just thinking – it's capturing your thoughts and turning them into reality.

*What have you been thinking about?*
How have you turned
those thoughts into actions?
How do you know when a
thought is complete?

**ANSWER:** You don't.

If you think you have a good thought or idea, just try it. Part of converting thoughts into actions is risk. The best way to look at risk is as *an opportunity to achieve and grow.*

**Set aside THINK! time.** Make a THINK! appointment every day, even if it's only 15 minutes. Decide in advance what you want to think about and what solutions you're looking for.

*I know it sounds hokey — but here's the gold:*

Write ideas no matter how far-fetched they sound – just write down your thoughts for ten minutes straight. Your stream-of-consciousness thinking will net you some amazing results.

# THINK!
## Do it for a week. The results will be so amazing, you'll do it for a lifetime.

— *Jeffrey Gitomer*

PRINCIPLE 2:

# Self-belief.

## (the most convincing characteristic of a person)

**"If the salesman himself has faith in the honesty of his goods, he will have little trouble in convincing his customers."**
*Frank Farrington*
*(This quote was taken from an underlined book in Patterson's library.)*

**"Self-belief is the most convincing characteristic to others, and THE most convincing characteristic to yourself."**
*Jeffrey Gitomer*

First, and above all, Patterson trained his people to believe in themselves as human beings *before* learning anything else about their job or their process. In 1923, the first page of *The Primer* explained the importance of self-belief. "You must believe in yourself. You must believe that you can do what you undertake, or you can never do it. Success in anything is up to each one of us individually."

Self-belief is the fulcrum point of success. It's the bridge between your personal attitude and enthusiasm and your ability to transfer confidence to others.

# Without belief in what you do and who you work for, your ability to engage others will be low.

As you try to grow a career, most people focus on product knowledge, interpersonal skills, maybe some networking-relationship skills, and little else. You leave out one of the two critical success elements for true achievement and fulfillment: self-belief (the other being positive attitude).

**HISTORY:** The common thread among all thought leaders, philosophers, and personal development experts is their consistent writing on the subjects of positive thinking and self-belief.

Dale Carnegie, author of the timeless *How to Win Friends and Influence People*, said, "If you believe in what you are doing, then let nothing hold you up in your work. Much of the best work of the world has been done against seeming impossibilities. The thing is to get the work done."

See what I mean? Well, is that you? How deep is your belief?

**CHALLENGE:** Timeless quotes are truths that have stood the test of time. The challenge with quotes is that most people (not you, of course) see them at a glance, fail to realize their power, and, worse, fail to take any action. Reading is not believing. Action dictates belief. Your words and actions are a mirror of your belief.

The reason these quotes and truths fail to take hold is that they require you to come to grips with yourself. They make you think about where you have been, where you are, and where you seek to grow.

Among hundreds of powerful thoughts and pearls of wisdom, Napoleon Hill, in his epic self-help book, *Think and Grow Rich*, said, "Whatever the mind of man can conceive and believe it can achieve." See the trend?

My inbox this morning had this "quote of the day" from Maxwell Maltz, author of *Psycho Cybernetics* – "Within you right now is the power to do things you never dreamed possible. This power becomes available to you just as soon as you can change your beliefs."

*How about you?*

- **What do you believe in?**

- **Do you believe enough to live with passion?**

- **Do you believe enough to convince others to see your point of view, or your way, as the best way?**

- **Do you believe enough to succeed?**

- **How can you strengthen your self-belief?**

- **Do you realize that self-belief is tied to your degree of success?**

"Mediocrity stems from lack of belief more than lack of skill." That's my quote. And, in my experience, I could not write words more true.

If you want to maximize your chances of increasing your success, deepen your belief system before you do anything else.

In order to do this, extreme self-evaluation must take place. It's not something you can learn in a seminar or a training session. It's something you can only give yourself. The key words are: "You Gotta Believe."

To discover "how," you must ask yourself "why." Why you believe or why you don't, and what you have to do in order to deepen yours.

 **Want a life changing lesson?** Write down the elements or things that are causing weakness on your beliefs. Then write the remedies and focus on them for the next year.

**HERE'S THE COOL PART:** The deeper your belief, the deeper your pockets. Strong belief will make you a more innovative, creative person with a burning drive and desire to help the other person and help them buy. There's a big difference between having a burning drive and having the desire to sell something. *People don't like to be sold, but they love to buy.*

# Free Git✗Bit...Want a few more quotes on belief?
Go to www.gitomer.com, register if you're a first-time visitor, and enter the words I BELIEVE in the GitBit box.

# Positive mental attitude is determined by you. Not others.

**"Success is up to the attitude within each one of us individually."**
*John Patterson*

**"The way you dedicate yourself to the way you think is the definition of attitude, either positive or negative. The only difference is the choice you make about the way you think."**
*Jeffrey Gitomer*

You convince yourself that life will be better after you get a better job, get more money, get married, have a baby, or some other "after." Then you are frustrated that the kids aren't old enough, and you'll be more content when they are. After that you're frustrated that you have teenagers to deal with. You will certainly be happy when they are out of that stage. You tell yourself that your life will be more complete when your spouse gets his or her act together, when you get a nicer car, a new house, a raise in pay, a new boss, or worse, when you retire.

**THE TRUTH IS:** There's no better time to be happy than right now. If not now, when?

Your life will always be filled with challenges, barriers, and disappointments. It's best to admit this to yourself and decide to be happy anyway.

Alfred Souza said, "For a long, long time it had seemed to me that I was about to begin real life. But there was always some obstacle in the way, something to be gotten through first, some unfinished business, time still to be served, a debt to be paid. Then life would begin. At last it dawned on me that these obstacles were my life."

Your mental attitude is your motivation and your inspiration.

Positive mental attitude is the motivation and inspiration that feeds off of your self-belief. Success in business, success in career, success in sales, success in service, AND success in LIFE starts with a positive attitude.

To put attitude in *your* perspective, I have gone beyond positive attitude and written *The Little Gold Book of YES! Attitude*. It's a book that heightens positive to a new level – the level of YES!

YES! thinking. YES! speaking. And taking YES! actions.

Attitude is defined as the way you dedicate yourself to the way you think. Think negative or think positive is a choice and a process. Negative is (unfortunately) an instinctive process. Positive is a learned self-discipline that must be studied and practiced every day.

**THINK!:** When you're giving any form of communication or presentation, your attitude will shine through.

Sometimes your personal sun is not shining. Things may be wrong with your family, finances, or your health.

If you let this transcend into your job, your business, your presentations, and your customer communications, the consequence is low or no sales, risk of losing customers, lower morale in the workplace, and a variety of other negative things.

And unless you have formalized attitude training, the result will be that you blame others for your own inability to separate your attitude from your events.

 **Want to start making an attitude change?** Take attitude actions. To achieve a positive attitude, you must take physical, verbal, and mental ACTIONS. Select a positive quote every day and send it to the 50 most important people in your life. After a few months, expand the list to your 50 most important business connections and customers. The results will enhance your attitude to the YES! level.

There is no one way
to happiness.
Happiness is the way.
It's inside your head FIRST
and everyplace else second.

So treasure every moment that you have. And treasure it more because you share it with someone special enough to invest your time...

Stop waiting until you finish school, until you go back to school, until you lose ten pounds, until you gain ten pounds, until you get married, until you have kids, until you quit smoking, or until your kids leave the house.

Stop waiting until you retire, until you get divorced, until Friday night, until Sunday morning, until you get your new car or home, until your car or home is paid off, until spring, until summer, until fall, until winter, or until the first or the fifteenth.

Stop waiting until your song comes on, until you've had a drink, until you've sobered up, until you win the lottery, or until the cows come home.

Decide today that there is no better time than *right now* to be happy.

# Happiness is now.
# Not a goal or a destination.

# Happiness is a daily choice.
# Decide to be happy.

**Free Git✗Bit...Want to know the 15.5 attitude actions to take that will help you on your path to happiness?** Go to www.gitomer.com, register if you're a first-time visitor and enter the words HAPPY ATTITUDE in the GitBit box.

# Boot camp separates the winner from the wanna-be winner.

"Industry is cheap. It is laziness that costs.
It has cost many a bright man a bright career."
*John Patterson*

"Business success is survival.
The well-prepared are most likely to survive,
the best-prepared are most likely to win."
*Jeffrey Gitomer*

Survival tactics, while they may not always be employed, must be mastered so that they can be implemented whenever the situation arises.

This is not simply how to find water in the desert; this is how to beat the competition, how to win when times are tough, and how to win in any struggle, or in any environment.

Survival is not about saving your hide; survival is about mastering a circumstance or environment and emerging victorious.

Survival is about being in shape, being ready, and being willing to act no matter what the situation, or the time of day.

# Basic training includes physical, mental, and psychological self-discipline. Intense basic training is a requirement for success in any sport, particularly the sport of business.

If you enter the army or any armed forces service, the first thing they do is get you in shape, physical shape, so that you can tackle the mental tasks. It's called boot camp. And anyone that's gone through it remembers every day of it. And whether they liked it or not, every one of them will admit that they were in their best shape at the end.

Patterson put his men through his own personal boot camp in order to ensure he was hiring only the BEST men for his team.

He didn't view the hiring process as hiring an employee or a salesman. Rather, he hired people who he planned to train in business, sales, and success.

The "basic training" that Patterson put his people through was more like army basic training. And he made people go through his basic training program in a tent, in a field, with hundreds of others, rain or shine, hot or cold, *before* they were hired – which ensured that he was hiring a strong person in every sense of the word.

His ability to attract the best was legendary. People were willing to come (and they came by the hundreds) to a Patterson camp and prove they could qualify to be an NCR employee before they ever earned a nickel. In 1900, starting pay was $4 a week.

But they didn't have to worry about gas money – there weren't any cars yet.

Have you ever noticed that some people look more alive than others? People who combine physical and mental exercise are more alert, ready to produce, ready to sell, and eager to serve. And by coincidence, they're also the ones whose enthusiasm and self-confidence are contagious.

And in business, it's those people whose information is better received – in a positive manner. I guess you could refer to it as the total package of brains, brawn, and beauty. Not "pretty." Rather "attractive." And that equates to believability and acceptance.

People gradually go from groove to rut because they fail to keep the intensity of basic training in their daily lives. How much energy are you putting into your basic training?

 **How dedicated are you to getting better at what you do?** What is your personal boot camp? How would you describe it? How do you discipline yourself? What is your daily agenda?

**CONSIDER THIS:** Would you have survived in Patterson's boot camp? Or would you have complained, "No cable TV?"

*The NCR Archive at the Montgomery Historical Society*
Tents at Sugar Camp training site, c1924.

Exercise should be both physical and mental. Working out can improve your business game. Train mentally for 30 minutes a day. Train physically for 30 minutes a day. Sweat a little. Give yourself those gifts for a lifetime.

Regular physical exercise can...

- **reduce your level of anxiety**
- **help manage stress more effectively**
- **improve your positive self-esteem and confidence**
- **help you relax and sleep more restfully**
- **teach you about goal-setting, dedication, and personal achievement**

There is a link between physical and mental fitness. Blood flow to the brain caused by physical exercise leads to clearer thoughts and better decisions. How can you *not* find 30 minutes, five times a week to fit all those physical benefits into your mental success plan?

**"Ill health affects the mental ability, spoils the disposition, and handicaps one's progress."**
*John Patterson*

**"Your physical status may be robbing you of a chance for fiscal success."**
*Jeffrey Gitomer*

*The NCR Archive at the Montgomery Historical Society*

NCR sales agents' training class, July 11, 1924.
Can you imagine your team out in the field doing this?
For a week? In the rain?

# Achieving is a blend of mental and physical symphonic motions that perform in harmony with each other. When your mind and body aren't working in unison, the performance is off-key.

*– Jeffrey Gitomer*

PRINCIPLE 5:

# Survival and success are a combination of knowing and doing.

"If there ever comes a time in this business when courage will not be necessary, when it will not be necessary for us to fight against obstacles, I shall know that it is time to put up the shutters, turn off the power, and draw the fires for all times."
*John Patterson*

"You already know what to do. Problem is, you're just not doing it."
*Jeffrey Gitomer*

"The biggest reason people don't succeed is that they don't expose themselves to existing information," says Jim Rohn.

And I add to that, "They don't believe in themselves enough (lack the confidence) to succeed."

It's not so important that you want to succeed – it's critical you know why you want to succeed, what has prevented you from achieving your success to date, and the belief system and game plan you are going to put in place to gain that success.

It's easy to lose self-belief if the one you've got in place is weak due to poor knowledge, lack of determination, and lack of love of what you do. It's easy to fail at your job if you've never told yourself (sold yourself) the real reason you want success in the first place. Not earning money for money's sake – but *the real reason you want the money* and *what you'll do with it once you get it.*

 **How do you continue to educate yourself? How much time do you dedicate to your own personal achievement?** (This will help you get to the "knowing" part.) How are you taking 15 minutes a day to learn new things about your attitude, your business, your sales skills, your customer service, and your life? Are you at home filling your brain with useless TV reruns?

# Or are you making the most of your time, *studying* to make yourself a better person, a better friend, a better spouse, a better parent, a better coworker, and a better businessperson?

**THINK!** about the questions on the following page. They may be painful at first, but if you can fill the gap between what your answers are and what your answers should be, that will provide the pathway to your success. (The "doing" part.)

1.  How many books have you read in the last year?

2.  How many books have you read on positive attitude or personal development in the last year?

3.  How many books have you read on creativity or thinking in the last year?

4.  How many hours did you waste watching television last week?

5.  Do you get paid for watching TV? Why are you watching?

6.  Could you convert or invest some of your "TV hours" into reading hours?

7.  How many personal development CDs do you listen to in your car?

8.  How many hours of radio drivel do you listen to in the car?

9.  How many hours could you convert or invest from drivel to knowledge?

10.  What would that conversion be worth?

10.5  What price are you paying for not converting spent time into invested time?

Survival and success is a combination of knowing and doing. What do you KNOW? How much do you know? How does that compare to what you NEED to know? What are you DOING with your time? What are you DOING to build your success?

The answers to those questions will lead you to the reality of where you are now and what you need to be DOING to get to the next level of success.

**KNOWING:** Why do you want to succeed? Each time you answer that question, add the question "Why?" After four or five levels, you'll have the real why.

**DOING:** Take the first 15 minutes of each day and DO something positive for yourself. This one small action will create a growth opportunity you may be cheating yourself out of.

**SURVIVAL:** Think about what you would do if you lost two of your best customers. Make a plan to prevent it before it becomes a reality.

**SUCCESS:** Meet with successful people once a week, and ask them each one question that may help you succeed. At the end of a year, you'll have 50 pieces of gold.

## What do you know? How are you turning that knowledge into money?

*The NCR Archive at the Montgomery Historical Society*

Patterson presenting to the "I Will" club, 1913.

**"The best way to teach is through the eye and the hand. It is hard to retain what we hear, but a man remembers what he sees and does."**
*John Patterson*

**"If you want to build wealth, first build a wealth of knowledge."**
*Jeffrey Gitomer*

PRINCIPLE 6:

# Studying. The first discipline of knowledge.

**"There are some young fellows who apparently think salesmanship is a thing that they will someday find somewhere ready-made."**
*John Patterson*

**"You don't get great at anything in a day, you get great at sales day by day."**
*Jeffrey Gitomer*

The word "studying" is a misnomer. It's actually personal development and knowledge expansion. It's education. Awareness. And the desire and dedication to want to learn.

## The difference between reading and studying is intensity, focus, and a willingness to act on what you have learned.

You must continually repeat messages and practice by doing in order to master the principles and the fundamentals that will lead to success.

# Studying is defined as the continuing self-discipline applied to achieve greatness.

On-the-job training is one of the most important facets of a successful company. You never stop learning, so why should you stop training to be your best?

Top athletes are constantly training to perfect their game and stay at peak performance. Top business people and salespeople need to do the same.

**ARE YOU SPENDING OR INVESTING YOUR TIME?** How many hours a day do you spend in front of the television? How is that helping your success? How else can you invest that time? What is going to help your success more: watching 30 minutes of reruns or dedicating 30 minutes to reading a book that will help the most important person in the world – YOU?

**Are you studying to be successful in business, or did you just think it would happen over time?** Business is complex, especially as it grows. The more you remain a student of business and your business, the more you study your market and your customers – the better chance you have for understanding, creating new ideas, differentiating yourself from the competition, and achieving success.

**THINK!** about how you learn. When you were in high school or college, how did you study for exams? How did you learn your material? Note cards, study groups, reading, being quizzed, cram, cheat, take notes?

**REALITY:** Those habits are still with you.

Business and sales are learned skills acquired by people with the attitude, aptitude, fortitude, desire, and the persistence and determination to succeed.

All of these skills are your personal development skills that must be incorporated with your business skills.

The formula is real simple: If you believe in your product, your service, your company, and yourself; if you work on yourself, reading the above subjects that you never learned in school; and you study the fundamentals of business, sales, attitude, and service from the rest of my books, you will begin to develop a self-confidence from learning and taking your own successful actions.

**HELP YOURSELF FIRST:** If your company does not have adequate training, create your own plan. All the information you need to succeed beyond your wildest dreams already exists. The problem is, you're not exposing yourself to it.

# Have you got the desire to learn the skills needed to succeed?

**HINT:** Fifty percent of that desire comes from loving what you do.

*Here's a self-test AND game plan:*

- **Do I spend 15 minutes a day reading or listening to success information?**

- **Do I know how other people's jobs at my office affect my job and my performance?**

- **Do I read the trade magazines of our company's industry and the trade magazines of our top five customers' industries?**

- **Do I attend our industry's annual trade show?**

- **Do I belong to Toastmasters?**

- **Where's my training "road map" taking me?**

 **Here's an idea!** Read about, study, or listen to one new business or success technique each day and before the end of the day, try that technique out at least once. By trying it, you'll see the real-world application of what you thought might work.

**BONUS:** If you practice one technique a day, at the end of one year, you'll have roughly 250 new techniques and still have your weekends free. At the end of five years, you'll be a world-class expert. Maybe *the* world-class expert.

# Business is nothing but teaching.

*— John Patterson*

# Invest time, don't spend it. Training takes time. But it's the best lifelong investment a person can make. Invest time in training yourself and others.

*— Jeffrey Gitomer*

PRINCIPLE 7:

# Your library is the artesian well of knowledge.

*"What a fine thing your brain is; your brain is a part of all it has met; hence, meet great men – you can meet them in books."*
*From NCR's* How To Close A Sale

*"Formal education will earn you a living, self-education will earn you a fortune."*
*Jim Rohn*

*"You determine how much of a fortune you want to earn by how much you decide to self-educate."*
*Jeffrey Gitomer*

It's difficult to read books if you don't own them. A library full of success books gives you the opportunity to gain the wisdom of others if you just employ this one word: READ.

If you want to discover the intimate thought patterns of someone else, take a close look at their library.

What they read usually determines how they think. If you decide to read about success, the odds are you will become successful. Your library is something to build upon to help you continue your studying.

John D. Rockefeller didn't use a library card. He endowed the library. **REASON?** He bought books and kept them instead of borrowing them for a week.

# Books are not just for reading. They are also for reference.

People often say to me, "I read that book." People rarely say to me, "I use the principles of that book every day." If you own the book, you have the chance to go back and refer to it for additional knowledge or clarification.

**THINK!** about reading. Start by reading books about things you love or are interested in. That will begin to create the habit and the thirst for knowledge. Knowledge, like any other addiction, is a drug. Fifteen beers? Or fifteen books? One will get you to the men's room, the other will allow you to own the men's room. Dedication to lifelong learning means reading and listening to something for your personal development at least an hour a day. Makes sense!

 **List the books you *have* read that improved your business, your sales, your attitude, and your life.** Then list the books you *should* be reading and what is stopping you from reading them.

I collect books on business, sales, personal development, and every aspect of success. Old books, some rare, some common, all good, all helpful, all with gems of knowledge.

# Training doesn't get you to the top of your plateau. Education does. Training teaches you how. Education teaches you WHY.

**@BAT:** Read three business or positive-attitude books at once, a chapter at a time. Write action notes and ideas in the margins of the book and bend the pages or transpose the information into your laptop at once. This assures that your knowledge and ideas will be acted upon.

**NOTE OF CAUTION ABOUT ATTITUDE BOOKS:** Old personal development books (Hill, Marden, Carnegie) are hokey. BUT they are equally valid. Idiots will pass them off as passé and not read them.

# Don't be an idiot!

**HERE'S WHAT I DO:** I read them. I devour them. I study their principles. And I live them every day.

**Free Git✗Bit…Want the list of books I suggest?** Go to www.gitomer.com, register if you're a first-time visitor, and enter the words BOOK LIST in the GitBit box.

# Planning prevents wandering and provides direction.

**"If you plan your work, you will not find yourself standing on the corner wondering where to go next."**
*John Patterson*

**"Goals are the road map that will direct you to success. But they don't guarantee success. You do."**
*Jeffrey Gitomer*

The same people who use road maps for traveling often omit road maps for goals and success. People like you.

I'm amazed at the number of people who use MapQuest or Google to print out a map to get from point A to point B. They do it all the time. But they (not you, of course) *never* map out and print out their goals before taking action toward achieving them.

A solid plan of attack for personal development (a map), more specific product knowledge, and new, bright ideas for market penetration and customer engagement will provide a faster, more successful result.

There's an old cliché that says, "If Moses had a map, he would not have had to wander for 40 years."

Everyone sets goals.

Some people set them on their own – others have them set for them (sales goals, sales plans, sales quotas). Some people make elaborate game plans for goal achievement, others write them down in their day planner, and others just cut out a picture from a magazine depicting something they wish they had, but don't (car, boat, house, vacation).

**Me?** I post my goals on my bathroom mirror. In plain sight.

**POST-IT NOTE YOUR WAY TO REAL ACHIEVEMENT:** I have developed the best, easiest method for achieving goals. Go get a pad of Post-it Notes. Write your goals on a dozen of them, big goals and small goals. Then stick them to your bathroom mirror.

By looking at them every morning and every evening, you will begin to take action. Achievement action. Just a little each day until one day your goal is achieved.

After you complete the achievement, take it off your bathroom mirror and post it on your bedroom mirror. Every day, as you get dressed, you can see (and relive) your success!

**Free GitBit**...**Get your Post-it Note goal achiever starter kit.** Want a preprinted pad of Post-it Notes to get started? I'd love to send you one in appreciation of your continued support and readership. **Send $1 to cover postage** to Buy Gitomer, 310 Arlington Ave, Loft 329, Charlotte, NC 28203.

Many passé seminar leaders and motivational speakers claim, "Less than four percent of all people set goals."

Baloney. Everyone has a goal, or many goals. If you're looking for a category that fits the four percent number, it's the people that actually *achieve* the goals they set.

### Ever set a goal you failed to achieve?

### Ever stop in the middle of a goal?

### Ever fall back to your old ways?

### Of course you have. Everyone has.

### Want to know why?

Enter Ali Edwards. And my personal biggest AHA! of the year. She has the answer.

On Ali's blog, www.aliedwards.typepad.com, she shared her thoughts, and what she's learned from others, when she asked her readers (me among them), "What are your intentions?" It was a WOW!, an AHA!, and a WAY COOL! all at the same time.

Goals and intentions are linked. Intentions actually precede goal setting. If you fall short of intention, you will not likely achieve the goal you set. What a simple, powerful concept. And what a truth.

Ali simply asks: *What are your intentions? What do you intend to do?* And the rest of the actions to achieve it will follow. Goals or intentions – which are more powerful?

You may have a goal, or you may have been given a goal, but your intentions will dictate the outcome of the effort (or lack of it). What do you intend to do?

*Think about these questions:*

## What do you want to do?

## What do you need to do?

## What do you have to do?

## What do you love to do?

## How much do you love what you do?

## Do you dislike what you do?

*Now, maybe you can better answer this question:*

## What do you INTEND to do?

What you intend to do are the thoughts behind your actions. Intentions are the justification behind your words and deeds. If you intend to manipulate, your words and deeds will follow. If your intentions are pure, your words and deeds will follow. If you intend to achieve your goals, or a specific goal, your words and deeds will follow.

I believe that love and intentions are connected more passionately than fear and intentions, or greed and intentions. There's an old quote that says, "The road to hell is paved with good intentions." I wonder how true it is. Personally, I believe the opposite.

There are types of intentions. The easiest to define are "good" and "bad." To intend to do the right thing, or intend to do the wrong thing. Sometimes your intention to do the wrong thing is justified by the way you feel. You believe someone "deserves" what you're about to do. I believe that's the "hell" intention.

Whatever your intentions are, they form the basis for your actions, the foundation for the achievement of your goals, the manifestation of your desires, and ultimately the fulfillment of your dreams.

Maybe you need to write down your intentions BEFORE you write your goals. Start each sentence with, "I intend to…" or even bolder, "By the end of the week, I intend to…" Timing your intentions makes them much more real.

Simply put, what you intend to do is what you actually do. Goals notwithstanding, it's all about your intentions.

 **An easy way to make your intentions clear is to categorize them.** Organize the categories – then write the words to define them. Use single words for categories and sentences to define your intentions. Use categories like personal, career, job, study, read, business, life, family, money, fun, travel, and passion. You get the idea.

Then write what you intend to do, and by when. "I intend by this date…" Short spaces of time are the best – this year – this month – this week – this day – this minute. What do you intend to do?

**THINK!** about your mission. A personal mission statement is your affirmation, philosophy, and purpose rolled into one. It's an opportunity to bring your goals into focus and transfer your ideals into the real world.

It's a chance for you to write your own legacy. It's your personal challenge to yourself. Sounds pretty heavy, but it's actually fun if you do it right.

Do you write down your goals? How many have you accomplished in the last month or year? What would help you meet your goals in the next 30 days? Six months? Or one year? Don't let your goals fall by the wayside (like your New Year's resolutions).

 **Direct yourself.** Each day, create one single direction that you must achieve, even if your ass falls off. Just one thing that at the end of each day makes you say, "I did it!" After a month, it will be easy to add one more thing. At the end of a year, you will be doing ten things a day and accomplishing them all.

**Free Git✗Bit...**If you'd like Ali Edwards' take on intentions, her essay and scrapbook on the subject which originally appeared in *Creating Keepsakes* magazine can be had by going to www.gitomer.com, registering if you're a first-time visitor, and entering the word ALI in the GitBit box.

# For everything that Patterson did, there had to be an objective. A goal. Everything he did was a step toward something bigger, better, best! Hence his primary principle, "Good enough is the enemy of all progress."

*– Jeffrey Gitomer*

# Use "today time management."

**"Nothing in business is as valuable as time."**
*John Patterson*

**"The successful person takes advantage of time all the time; the unsuccessful person laments in the lack of it."**
*Jeffrey Gitomer*

Every person has the same amount of time.

A wise investment of time is the best non-monetary investment you can make. Time management is intuitive for some, but it can also be a learned process.

## The basic underlying principle of time management is "do what's important first."

Patterson had a "things to do today" chart which hung on the wall in his office. It was very big, so there was no way he could avoid it. Patterson wanted to make sure that all tasks, large or small, were completed in the time frame given. If they were, he knew he had a productive day. He believed in this time management strategy for his salesmen and for the executives of NCR.

Time management is not complicated – unless you take a time management course. Then you have to have a minor degree in rocket science to figure out what piece of paper gets what notes in what category and with what priority.

 **Create Post-it Notes with the day's tasks.** At the end of the day, check off the ones that you completed. If you didn't accomplish any, you didn't have a productive day.

# Time management is instinctive. You already know what to do. Your problem is not doing it.

**THINK!** about time management. If you prioritize all your "A projects," "B projects," and "C projects," never do a B project until you've completed all your As.

People make the mistake of getting the little things out of the way before they tackle the big things. Get the big things out of the way first, and the little things will disappear.

**QUESTION:** Why can't people get things done?

**ANSWER:** They don't know the difference between urgency and importance.

Everyone has "no time." That's baloney – everyone has the same amount of time, it just depends whether they spend it or invest it. If you're not in your "A project" list or preparing something for your "A project" list, you're pretty much wasting your time.

What people do with their time is "piss on fires." They do what's urgent, but not what's important, and there's a big difference. When they're doing something important, an "A project," and then something urgent comes up, it takes away from their important time. I think it is imperative to understand the difference between *urgency* and *importance*.

Someone barges into your door and says, "Hey we gotta do this right now!" *That's urgent.* A customer calls on the phone and you shipped them the wrong order or it didn't arrive on time. It's lost on a truck someplace. It's backordered, and they weren't expecting it to be backordered. *That's urgent.*

## Most urgent things are preventable – even heart attacks.

*Important* things are things that build yourself, or your career, or your business, or your family. Actions that help you achieve your goals. They're more long-term things.

Do you have to take care of the urgent things? Of course you do. You also have to deal with the important things of the day. For example, I've got a proposal right now that I'm doing for a big customer. It will lead me to a ten-year relationship with them.

## It's both urgent *and* important because there's a deadline attached to it.

The problem with most people is that they fail to balance their use of time because they think they MUST handle every urgent matter themselves. Big mistake. And big misuse of time.

It's not just a problem for you. It's a problem for me as well. I, like you, think I'm the best person to handle each problem. Finally, after a decade of frantic running around, I decided to guard my time.

I try to schedule my time so that it gives me full use of each hour of the day. I want to write that proposal during time when I have the benefit of clear and energized thought, instead of being forced to do it in the middle of the heat of all the other crap.

Sometimes I'll leave where I am to find a place of solitude. As an example of that, I've thrown myself out of my own office. I don't even have a desk there. I work out of my home office because of the peace and comfort I find there.

My library is there, and only a few people know my phone number there. In my office, I don't screen calls. If anyone in the world calls, I take their call no matter what. I don't want to change that so, out of fairness to me, I've decided that I'm going to be in the office less frequently. I don't want to lie to somebody and tell them I'm not there if I'm there. That's not right.

I discovered a secret in my life that was huge. Most people think they're evening people, and they're wrong. What they're saying is, "I ruin myself in the evening, and I can't get up in the morning."

**HERE'S A CLUE:** Schedule time with space for clarity.

**DAY OR NIGHT?** I thought I was an evening person for 43 years. But I can do the most in the morning when I'm clear. And so can you.

Been doing too much working in the evening? Or drinking too much wine? Or eating too much food? Or staying up too late? Or watching too much television?

**HERE'S WHAT TO DO:** Go to bed an hour earlier. Wake up an hour earlier in the morning. Do some kind of exercise, either mental or physical.

There's a step in the middle. Make certain that when you go to sleep your head is clear. Write down everything that you need to do, all the projects you've got, and everything you're thinking about. Just write it all down. If you write it all down, you're in great mental shape.

Make a to-do list for the next day and a to-do list for the next month. Make a project list or an idea page. Anything you've gotta do. It'll allow you to wake up with solutions instead of waking up thinking about your problems.

 **Get in front of people who can say "Yes" or help you.** This is the single highest priority and most productive use of your time. The time you spend with the right people is in direct proportion to the number of successes you will have.

**Time management is not the process. Time investment is a better way to look at it. How will you invest your time today, and what's the return on your investment?**
*Jeffrey Gitomer*

# THE NEXT 10 PRINCIPLES ARE ABOUT SELLING AS IT RELATES TO BUSINESS SUCCESS.

They will challenge you to think about sales and selling as a key-to-success function, and how the elements of sales spill over to every aspect of business.

I have a thousand emails from people reading my sales books that start out: "I'm not actually in sales, but I love your book because it relates to my job and my life, not just selling."

If you're "not exactly in sales" these next 10 principles are just as important as the rest of the book.

Read them, enjoy them, learn from them, and profit from them.

# Prospect for probable purchasers to build your business organically.

**"Take it for granted that everyone can buy, rather than determining without an interview that some people will not buy."**
*John Patterson*

**"Put yourself in front of people who can say yes to you."**
*Jeffrey Gitomer*

Every business wants more customers.

**THE CHALLENGE IS:** Where are they, AND are they ready to buy when they're exposed to your message or your advertisement? Businesses will spend huge amounts of money to introduce their company, product, or message to potential customers. The search for customers is the same as the search for gold. Every early prospector was in search of a gold mine. "Gold fever," they called it. They would pay any amount of money for the map that would lead them to the gold. Many paid with their lives.

Nowadays, prospecting for new customers and probable purchasers is not as dangerous, but is equally as rewarding. And how to prospect is equally as important as where to prospect. Or better stated *proper prospecting prevents poverty*.

Prospecting was and still is an important part of earning the sale and building a business. NCR salesmen were given a territory and were expected to earn a sale from all businesses in that territory. As each salesman traveled through a town, they were expected to stop at every local business and call on every merchant.

However, prospecting was much more difficult in the 1900s because of the lack of technology. Salesmen couldn't do much pre-call research on the company they wanted to call on. They couldn't look online. They couldn't send an e-mail to someone in the company. They had to talk to nearby store owners or others in town who might know the probable purchaser they wanted to call on.

As NCR grew, prospecting became easier for the salesmen because of the number of referrals that were made. Looking for new probable purchasers? Who isn't? You probably have hundreds you're not paying attention to. Like your present customers!

Your present customers already know you and like you; you have established rapport, confidence, and trust; you know they have good credit because they have paid you in the past; and you know they will return your call.

I don't think you have to ask for much more than that.

Your best NEW prospects are your existing customers. They will buy more, and *if the relationship is there*, they will refer you to others.

**THINK!** about how you're different. What separates you from the businesses that offer the same products or services that you do?

The best way to start this discovery process is ask your present customers why they chose you rather than others. This will help you significantly when you try to get new customers. Once you know the reasons that others have done business with you, it gives you both confidence and dialog when engaging someone new.

*Here are your personal affirmations for attracting new customers and probable purchasers:*

**I Work Hard.** "Work only half a day. It makes no difference which half, the first 12 hours or the last 12 hours," said Kemmons Wilson, the founder of Holiday Inn.

**I Bring Solid Value.** Provide something of value that will benefit the probable purchaser that your competition cannot match.

**I Am Responsive.** Try to always exceed your customers' expectations in all contacts you may have with them. Customers want you to get to the point, and they want you to get there fast.

**I Am a Straight Shooter.** Build a reputation as an honest person. Tell the truth, and you don't have to worry about what you say coming back to haunt you.

**I Build a Great Reputation.** Do the right things consistently and you will build a reputation that precedes you. Your reputation will make it easier for you to continue to work with your existing customers and to prospect new customers. If you have a bad reputation, good luck getting rid of it!

**I Listen to Understand.** If you are not so busy doing all of the talking, your customers in most cases will tell you exactly what they want and what you need to do to "get the business."

**I Keep My Customers In Front of My Face. And I Keep Myself In Front of Their Face – Every Week.** My medium is my weekly column in newspapers across the U.S. and my global, weekly e-zine. My medium is my weekly column in newspapers around the U.S. and my global, weekly e-zine. My e-zine is value-packed and information-loaded. And it provides the reader an opportunity to purchase my varied offerings such as books, CDs, online training, or tickets to a public event. They're presented in a low-key manner. And the value of my sales information is the prominent offering.

Whatever your position is in the company, keep your key customer list on your desk. If you have not spoken with one of them in a while, pick up the phone before your competition does.

**I Follow Through.** Say what you will do, and do what you say you will do. Follow-through develops reputation. So do dropped balls.

 **@BAT: Call ten customers a day.** Ask them why they continue to do business with you. Write it down. Ask for a referral, and ask for more business. Put down the book and call one NOW!

PRINCIPLE 11:

# Increase business connections to increase sales.

*"A good plan is to have your agents assemble ... and have each one explain to you his methods of selling and the arguments he uses ... a convention of this sort will put dollars into your pocket."*
*John Patterson*

*"Networking is creating momentum toward business and career success."*
*Jeffrey Gitomer*
*from* The Little Black Book of Connections

In order for you to build your business, networking and connecting aren't just necessary, they're imperative.

## Patterson was a proponent of business people interacting with one another.

Trade shows, conventions, business meetings, seminars, and business gatherings of all kinds. He was able to make sales in any social environment. From banquets to ballgames. From picnics to presidential retreats.

John Patterson understood that business was not simply completed at a sales call or in an office, and that often his biggest deals were made in non-business environments or during atypical business hours.

The same as they are today.

*Here are the 5.5 basic rules of relationship-based networking from my* Little Black Book of Connections:

1. **Go where your best customers, probable purchasers, and prospects go.**

2. **Give value first. Be known as a resource.**

3. **Dig in. Be committed or it won't work.**

4. **Be consistent. Once you get involved, seek a leadership position.**

5. **Get to know people on a friendly basis.**

5.5 **Go slow. Relationships are not built in a day. They're built, with value, day-by-day.**

People tend to do business with people they trust. Be sincere, be yourself, and, over time, you will win their business and more.

 **@BAT: List five places where your best customers or probable purchasers go.** Go there. Have breakfast, have dinner, have fun with your probable purchaser and you will build a basic platform upon which they will *want* to do business with YOU.

PRINCIPLE 12:

# Creating the demand converts selling to buying.

*"If the prospect understood the proposition, he would not have to be sold; he would come to buy."*
*John Patterson*

*"People don't like to be sold, but they love to buy."*
*Jeffrey Gitomer*

**QUESTION:** How many people are calling you up on the phone and proactively asking to buy your product or service? The answer is: Not enough.

**DEEPER QUESTION:** What are you doing to create that demand? The answer is: Not enough.

John Patterson's objective was not to sell cash registers. Rather, he created the demand for a receipt. He encouraged people at every possible moment, in all his literature, in all his advertising, to "ask for a receipt." This message reached merchants without cash registers and provoked thought in a manner that produced the desire to purchase his machines.

## Desire leads to demand.

**Ask For a Receipt**

**This Registers the Amount of Your Purchase**

**Notice: Money Must be REGISTERED Before Goods Are Wrapped**

**The Company's Name (Personalized Receipt)**

**Amount Purchased**

At the top of each machine, Patterson put a marketing message. First it was "Ask For a Receipt." And later it was "Amount Purchased" so people could confirm the total on the receipt with the amount displayed on the register.

Every customer who walked by an NCR cash register saw a marketing message. The more often people saw the message, the more Patterson's business grew.

**DEEPEST QUESTION:** What message are you sending every time a customer makes a purchase from you?

*In order for your business to grow, you must:*

1. **Create the desire or the want.**

2. **Create the need or the demand.**

3. **Prove the need. Fill the demand.**

Don't just sell the product.

 **List five values (not benefits or features) that a customer receives in doing business with you.** If you can't, the best way to generate a 100% accurate list is to ask your five best customers.

**THINK!** about why you buy things for yourself. Is it a NEED or a WANT? Patterson was the first to understand that buying was an emotional process. You must create a balance between the emotion to trigger the desire and the logic to justify the purchase.

# Demand comes from desire. Desire comes from perceived value or gain.

You've seen it at Christmastime. The craze for the newest toy. The average consumer can't get enough of it (fast enough). That's demand. If you could do the same for your business, it would be a much easier life than the one you've got.

 **@BAT: Get your people and advisors together for a brainstorming or idea generation session.** Begin to create reasons why people would demand more of your product or service. Once you have 10 or more reasons why people would demand more of what you sell, then bring in 10 of your customers. Feed them well. Honor them. And ask them to participate in the same dialog.

Do not reveal your initial brainstorming list until after your customer's have shared their ideas. Then compare lists and begin an interactive dialog that will not only create new ideas, it will create new business.

PRINCIPLE 13:

# A prepared demonstration means personalized.

**"Don't go out shooting until you have your ammunition ready."**
*John Patterson*

**"A fumbling, excuse-making, apologizing salesperson builds zero confidence."**
*Jeffrey Gitomer*

Every customer who buys your product or uses your service wants to feel that it fits their need and their desire exactly. As a businessperson or a salesperson, your job is to tailor your message to fit their desire or need.

Seems simple at the core. But most salespeople are only halfway prepared to give a sales presentation or sales demonstration. They know many things about themselves and their product, but not enough about how the potential customer profits or produces from the use of his or her products and profits enough to purchase whatever you're selling without hesitation.

This is not caused by lack of preparation, but by lack of *proper* preparation.

If you want to give a great presentation, it must be both personalized – meaning that it's in terms of the customer's needs, not in terms of what you offer – and it must be different from and better than your competition.

If your presentation is perceived by the probable purchaser as relatively the same as your competition, then all that will matter is your price. If your presentation combines personalization and differentiation, you can win the sale on value.

Differentiation is achieved by being certain that you ask questions and make statements that your competition does not ask or say. Differentiation is making the customer feel they win when they purchase. Differentiation is adding humor. Differentiation is adding creativity to your presentation. Differentiation is being friendly. Differentiation is making certain the customer understands how your product or service will perform after they take ownership.

The combination of personalization and differentiation is a formula that will lead to sales. Lots of sales.

**NOTE:** Failure does not come from lack of sales; failure comes from lack of preparation.

Outcomes are predetermined, if you prepare.

**THINK ABOUT IT:** Isn't it worth the ten minutes it takes to make the sale easy? As they say in Boy Scouts, "If you ain't ready and rehearsed, you won't get the merit badge."

How well do you prepare for your presentation?

PRINCIPLE 14:

# Gain interest with information about the customer.

## (Not your company, your product, or you.)

**"Always leave him (the merchant)
in such a frame of mind that he will
be glad to have you call again."**
*John Patterson*

**"Product knowledge is useless until you know
how your product is used on the job to benefit
and create profit for the customer."**
*Jeffrey Gitomer*

In order to arouse the interest of a probable purchaser, it is the responsibility of the company to present compelling messages and the salesperson to be equally interesting.

The best ways to gain the interest of the potential customer are to share methods and strategies for profitability and productivity, share stories of how other customers have successfully done it, and save the boring (non-interesting) details for later.

Because the cash register wasn't something that everyone thought they needed at first, NCR salesmen had to find a way to gain the attention of a merchant before trying to pitch the sale. Patterson believed in these five steps to get the merchant interested.

*Five Steps in Interesting the Merchant (from* The Primer*):*

1. **Use indirect ways of interesting the merchant.**

2. **Call on the merchant.**

3. **Secure necessary information and study the store systems.**

4. **Get the merchant to realize weak points in his current system.**

5. **Make a definite appointment.**

**FAST FORWARD ONE HUNDRED YEARS:** In my experience, I have found that if a customer wants to know about my product, he or she will ask. You have a responsibility to gather information about the prospective customer so that your message is meaningful.

# If you have taken an interest in them, they will take an interest in you.

**How much talking does the prospective customer do when you and he meet?** The answer is in DIRECT PROPORTION to a sale being made. If the prospect talks 20% of the time, you have a 20% chance of making the sale.

How many PROFIT ideas are you bringing with you? The more ideas, the more likely the sale.

**MAJOR CLUE:** The probable purchaser is most interested in *his* benefit from buying your product or service.

Use the "You" method, not the "I" method. Talk about your probable purchaser's interests rather than your own if you want to keep his attention.

The more you know about them, the easier it is to get them to buy. If you bring your knowledge about the prospect, and how they profit from use – not how they save, but how they profit – the more likely it is that they will buy from you.

 **@BAT: Videotape yourself giving a sales presentation.** How many "we-we phrases" are you using? Are you boring your probable purchaser with drivel about your company? If someone were giving YOU this presentation, how long would it take for you to fall asleep? Now count the number of times you specifically address the needs and concerns of the probable purchaser. Ouch! Are you even connecting with them? Take note and take heart – and change your presentation.

# If you walk in with information about you, they consider you a salesman.

# If you walk in with ideas and answers, they consider you a resource.

# Which one are you?

*– Jeffrey Gtomer*

# Questions lead to answers. Answers lead to harmony. Answers lead to productivity. Answers lead to customers.

"Questions ... may start a train of thought
that will lead to good results."
*John Patterson*

"Questions are the heart of the thought process
and the engagement process."
*Jeffrey Gitomer*

In 1888, Sherlock Holmes stated, "It is a capital offense to theorize before one has data." This was actually said by Holmes on behalf of Sir Arthur Conan Doyle.

Questions breed dialog among people trying to agree or reach a goal. Questions can create more harmony than statements or directives.

Almost all arguments can be avoided if you ask a question of clarity or experience BEFORE you make a definitive (opinionated) statement.

In business, this is especially valuable because most people, at whatever job level, are seeking answers to help them do their job better. As a leader or even a co-worker, you have to know what your fellow workers are thinking and doing before you barge in with a statement.

# The right questions (non accusatory) will lead you to information and agreement.

In sales, preparing the proper questions will also lead to answers in which the prospective purchaser will convince himself that he is making the right decision to buy your product. The proper questions will lead to answers that bind and gain the respect of others, and to potential profit with probable purchase.

### Want to get others to think?
All you have to do is ask the right questions.

### Want to get others to act?
All you have to do is ask the right questions.

### Want to get others to respond?
All you have to do is ask the right questions.

### Want to get others to purchase?
All you have to do is ask the right questions.

The secret to questioning is to get the person to say (or think), "I've never been asked that before."

The questions that NCR salesmen were taught to ask challenged their probable purchaser to think about their business and the financial system it currently used to guard their cash received.

Questions such as, "Do you know exactly how much money was received in the last business day? Do you know exactly how much money went out in the last business day? Do you know that your employees are 100% accurate when opening the cash box and collecting and receiving money?"

These questions created the perceived value and demand for the register and showed the customer the value in owning one – without ever mentioning the product. Cha-Ching!

Patterson saw that in the process of building a business and selling his cash registers, questions helped create the demand, let the potential customer see the value in the product, gave the salesman valuable information about the probable purchasers business and needs, and helped him close the sale. Any questions?

What can the proper power questions do for you? And how are you mastering your questioning skills?

 **Make a list of 25 great questions.** The most powerful questions you can create. Study them, use them, refine them, and always have them at your fingertips.

*Here are 7.5 preparation success strategies for questioning:*

1.  Ask the probable purchaser questions that make him evaluate new information.

2.  Ask questions that qualify needs.

3.  Ask questions about improved productivity, profits, or savings.

4.  Ask questions about company or personal goals.

5.  Ask questions that separate you from your competition – not compare you to them.

6.  Ask questions that make the customer or probable purchaser think before giving a response.

7.  Ask questions to create a BUYING atmosphere – not a selling one.

7.5  A critical success strategy: To enhance your listening skills, write down answers. It proves you care, preserves your data for follow-up, keeps the record straight, and makes the customer feel important.

**@BAT: Ask the wrong questions, get the wrong answers.** Here's the ultimate challenge: Get one probable purchaser to say, "No one ever asked me that before."

PRINCIPLE 16:

# Listening leads to understanding.

**"Don't talk for the sake of talking.
Do listen for the sake of understanding"**
*John Patterson*

**"Listening is one of the most important aspects
of the communicating process, yet it's usually
the weakest part of a businessperson's
skill set – especially a sales professional."**
*Jeffrey Gitomer*

There are two basic kinds of listening: listening with the intent to respond, and listening with the intent to understand.

Listening with intent to respond leads to interruption. This principle focuses on the science of using both disciplines in the order of understanding FIRST and responding SECOND.

Here's a two-word lesson on listening – it's the best way to be certain your listening skills are as good as your selling skills – and those two words are not "Shut up!" The two words are: Take notes.

Note-taking makes listening a certainty and it lets your coworkers and customers know that their words are valuable enough to write down.

Are you a talker or a listener? Learn to be as good at shutting up and note taking as you are at talking.

 **When you leave a meeting, does your recollection of it ever differ from the person who was sitting right next to you?** Maybe it's because you were distracted – most likely it's because you didn't take notes.

Ever catch yourself formulating the next words to come out of your mouth rather than listening to the person until they were done speaking?

Sure you have – it's human nature. Don't do that.

*Here's a method toward error-free positive communication:*

1. **Listen without distractions.**

2. **Focus eye contact on the communicator.**

3. **Write the communication down.**

4. **Repeat it back or ask about it.**

5. **Get confirmation that you understand.**

5.5 **Deliver what you promised.**

 **@BAT: Learn how to be a better listener by asking a question at the end of their statement.** If you make a statement, it's possible that you were interrupting. But with a question, you almost *have* to wait until they're finished speaking.

PRINCIPLE 17:

# Less sell-talk-time lead to more-buy-time.

**"Don't talk all the time.
Give the merchant a chance."**
*John Patterson*

**"If you listen better, you will sell more."**
*Jeffrey Gitomer*

The balance between letting the other person talk and you talking must be weighed heavily in favor of the other guy. Most salespeople make the fatal mistake of selling when, in fact, the more the probable purchaser talks, the more they will sell themselves on the product or service.

The salesperson's responsibility is to create ways to let the probable purchaser have more talk time.

This is done through powerful questioning and powerful listening. The more powerful the question, the more the "probable purchaser" becomes a "profitable customer."

Salespeople think they have to "sell" to make the sale, and nothing could be further from the truth. If you let the customer talk long enough, they will see the purpose and value of saying yes. They will sell themselves.

**Questions and listening go hand in hand.** The only person who loses by having poor listening skills is you! How are you listening? Do you know how and when to be quiet? You can learn a lot from your customers if you give them the chance to talk!

*Look for these two symptoms of lousy listeners:*

- **A person who seems to have all the answers usually isn't listening.**

- **A person who interrupts isn't listening (or at least is not a good listener).**

**@BAT: Ask every customer a two-part question that when answered would be a reason to buy.** First ask what their experience has been. Let them talk. Then ask why they are buying now and what they hope to gain as a result of purchase. Let them talk more.

# This exercise will give the probable purchaser maximum talk time – and give you maximum understanding of their situation.

PRINCIPLE 18:

# Your message must be as compelling as your product to engage anyone – especially your customer.

**"You interest people, first, by the thing you talk about; and second, by the way you talk."**
*Manual for NCR Salesmen*

**"The secret to communication is not just engagement, it is INTELLIGENT, EMOTIONAL, FRIENDLY engagement."**
*Jeffrey Gitomer*

The key to any communication rests in how well you engage the other person or the audience.

Your preparation, the questions you ask, the ideas you bring, your communication and presentation skills, and your positive attitude and enthusiasm are the keys to intelligent engagement.

The old adage is, "It's not what you say – it's how you say it." Wrong. In business it's both. Making a great presentation is a marriage of "what you say" and "how you say it."

The list below concentrates on *how you say it*. If you deliver the greatest presentation in the world with no enthusiasm, sincerity, or belief – you'll lose.

*In the beginning of a presentation, there are 5.5 elements that determine whether a sale will be made or not:*

1. **Rapport.** Putting yourself on the same side of the fence with the probable purchaser. Finding something in common.

2. **Need.** Determining what the probable purchaser deems as the factors that will influence their motivation to listen and understand with the intent to purchase.

3. **Importance.** The weight that a probable purchaser assigns to a product, feature, benefit, price, or time frame.

4. **Confidence.** Your ability to gain credibility. Your ability to remove all doubt. Your ability to gain comfort that the risk of purchase will be less than the reward of ownership.

5. **Value Transferred.** Your ability to get the probable purchaser to perceive that he gains the most value by buying your product or service AND you are the most valuable person to buy it from.

5.5 **Enthusiasm.** Your belief, your attitude, and your passion in presenting your message makes it attractive enough to act upon.

While all of the information from these elements can be acquired by asking the right power questions, the difference between good and great salespeople is the way they present (deliver) their message.

**IT'S THE SAME IN YOUR BUSINESS.** Your ability to present a compelling, believable, enthusiastic, value-driven message is the difference between yes and no, understanding and confusion, acceptance or rejection, and even approval or denial.

Your bank line of credit, your delivery from a vendor, and the morale in your office all stem from your communication.

In sales, if you engage the probable purchaser with enthusiasm and value, you create an atmosphere to buy. If the engagement is still there at the end of the meeting, the probable purchaser is eager to buy.

Much is said about sales techniques used to coerce or persuade people to buy. Not much is said (or written) about presentation skills – fundamental communication competence, combined with public speaking adeptness to blend a symphonic (sales) pitch.

Your speaking skills must be used throughout the entire presentation, but they're critical at the start because they create an impression, and set a tone, for the rest of the meeting.

Real engagement is the most difficult part of selling because the salesperson (you) is unprepared to engage.

Oh, you may be prepared to sell – (insert crap about you and your product) – but you are ill-prepared to engage (stuff about the customer and how he profits from purchase).

No two sales presentations are alike, even if you're selling the same product and work for the same company.

Making a presentation is complex even if you're selling paper clips, and it's delicate even if you're selling 18-wheel trucks. Everyone has a different style of selling, *but* the elements of content and process in a presentation must be the same. You master the elements, and then adapt them to your style. It's what you say (the elements) combined with how you say it (your style).

**@BAT: Substitute television with sales-call preparation.** Give up TV for two nights a week and take that time to prepare questions that will engage the probable purchaser, gather valuable information that that customer will be respectful of and responsive to, and create several ways to ask for the sale. I promise you it will put more money in your pocket than watching your favorite show.

**Free Git✗Bit**...**Want the 10.5 ways to prepare for your sales presentation so you can be sure to win the sale?** Go to www.gitomer.com, register if you're a first-time visitor and enter the words WIN THE SALE in the GitBit box.

# An objection is the gateway to a sale.

**"An objection is nearly always an advantage to the salesman... to turn the objection into a real reason for buying."**
*John Patterson*

**"The selling process starts when the customer objects."**
*Jeffrey Gitomer*

I have always referred to objections of any kind – sales, business, or life – as "barriers." I believe this helps in the understanding of what it really is. Lower or remove the barrier, and victory is yours.

The biggest barrier in sales is not "money" as most people think. The biggest barrier in sales – maybe also in business and in life – is "risk" – taking it deeper – "unspoken risk." Real or perceived, if the risk is too high, no positive action will be taken.

Objections have been around since sales started. The training manual *Selling Helps for NCR Salesmen* prepared all of Patterson's men with answers to any objection they might encounter. Patterson saw objections as windows to more sales, and he was right. If a merchant objected to price, quality, service, or anything else, it was at this moment the salesman would qualify the product, show the value, and at the same time, create confidence in the buyer.

The NCR salesmen were prepared for objections. Are you? Each salesman knew exactly how to respond to every doubt in the merchant's mind. Maybe that's why the company is still around 120 years later. How many sales are you losing because you aren't prepared to overcome objections or lower the barriers? Answer: Too many.

Objections or barriers actually indicate interest and the need for more clarification or more proof on the part of the other person, and your responsibility is to provide proof, and do it enthusiastically.

Look forward to objections. Look forward to barriers. They are an indication of interest. They are the gateway to a sale.

**MAJOR CLUE**: If you can overcome an objection in your presentation, before anyone raises it, you are more likely to make a sale.

Business barriers are the same as sales barriers. They are risk or concern driven. They appear from employees, vendors, bankers, lawyers, Uncle Sam, and everyone in between. They must be answered, lowered, or removed so that progress can be made.

Look at them as challenges to your success and peace of mind. Small barriers can be answered, lowered, or overcome at the moment they appear. Big barriers require thought. Don't be afraid to ask for time to respond. Often the answers become obvious when the heat of the moment passes.

*Here are 6.5 steps to identify the true sales barrier (objection)*
*and how to overcome it:*

1. **Listen to the objection and decide if it's true.**

2. **Qualify it as the only one.**

3. **Confirm it again in a different way.**

4. **Qualify the objection to set up the close.**

5. **Answer the objection so that it completely resolves the issue and confirms the resolve.**

6. **Ask a closing question and communicate to the probable purchaser in an assumptive (I have the sale in hand) manner.**

6.5 **Confirm the answer and the sale in writing.**

**@BAT: List your ten biggest sales barriers.**
Create answers in a way that you can answer
them *before* they occur. Add ways to lower
them or answer them if they occur after your
presentation. You know they're coming, so why
not be ready to answer them in a creative way?

**Free GitⵣBit**...**Want to know the eight personal barriers
caused by YOU?** Go to www.gitomer.com, register if
you're a first-time visitor, and enter the word BARRIER in
the GitBit box.

# Selling is not manipulating; selling is harmonizing.

**"The successful salesman must learn to be all things to all people."**
*John Patterson*

**"Understand how your product is used (not just what it does) so you can understand how to harmonize with your prospect, sell it most effectively, and grow your business."**
*Jeffrey Gitomer*

I'm certain you have seen or heard the information about "typing" people. Driver, amiable, creative, whatever. And then you're told ways of manipulating what you do or say to be able to communicate with them.

Go back to the Dale Carnegie book *How to Win Friends and Influence People*, and you'll see the two words that explain harmony: "Be yourself."

And as you read this book, please note that EVERYTHING I am saying about the selling process applies to business as well. It's just more pronounced in selling because more persuasion is involved.

Selling is about understanding the other person. Each person has different motives to buy based on personality and needs. Salespeople cannot give the same presentation all the time. You've got to adapt the presentation to meet the needs and the personality of the potential customer without compromising your standards or altering your personality to a point where you have to remember the way you acted or spoke.

Patterson changed the register models presented to fit the customer personality type, not just their business type. This innovation made the product seem custom-fit.

I'm against systems of selling. They teach you a way, usually a manipulative way. And you gotta use that way. The problem is the probable purchaser may not want to buy that way. *Which way do you sell?*

Why people buy is ONE BILLION times more powerful than how to sell. One of the least known, and least deployed, skills in the science of selling is understanding the need and desires of the customer, their motive to buy. Buying motives are uncovered by asking questions.

Harmony is understanding, sensing the tone and comfort level of the customer, and using your character skills and interpersonal skills to harmonize.

Your job is to take the characteristics of the probable purchaser and blend them with the reason they are buying so that it motivates them to act and gives them enough confidence to buy.

**THINK!** about harmony in music. Your notes blend with other notes to create harmony.

Think of it the same way in sales. Think of it the same way in business.

# Are you in sync with your coworkers and your customers?

*Are you in-tune or off-key?*

*Here are a few guidelines that will work in any environment:*

1. **Never argue.**

2. **Never offend.**

3. **Never think or act like you are defeated.**

4. **Try to make a friend at all costs.**

5. **Try to get on the same side of the fence (harmonize).**

5.5 **Never have to remember what you said. (A. Write it down. B. Don't lie.)**

**@BAT: Write down the last five conflicts you had.** Then write down how you could have avoided them. Try your solutions the next time the same conflict situation arises.

PRINCIPLE 21:

# Complete the sale with an agreement to buy and be certain to give them a receipt.

**"Closing the sale is getting the probable purchaser's decision to buy."**
*John Patterson*

**"Assume the sale."**
*Jeffrey Gitomer*

Most salespeople are willing to walk away from a sales situation without an answer regarding the probable purchaser's intent to purchase.

The true probable purchaser will have no objection to being asked to purchase. Many times a salesperson is in the middle of a selling cycle, gets a buying signal, asks for the sale, and gets it. I refer to it as the principle of "One YES! leads to another."

**PATTERSON HAD IT RIGHT:** It's not "closing" the sale, it's "completing" the sale. Huge difference. Closing is pushing. Completing is the last step in the process of buying.

**HARD QUESTIONS:** How do you complete the sale? What is your selling cycle time? What could you do to make it sooner?

**ANSWER:** Ask for the sale sooner!

How many meetings, presentations, or phone calls does it take you to complete the sale?

**REMEMBER:** You are the *salesperson* and the probable purchaser is *expecting* you to ask for the sale. Don't disappoint him or her.

*Here are 5.5 effective closing strategies and tactics:*

**1. Challenge the probable purchaser to do what's best for his business.** This strategy is great when the customer is doing business with an existing vendor or friend who is not providing the best product or service.

**2. You are an expert at what you do.** And the customer can have peace of mind to do what he does best, knowing your part of your job will get done. Always let the customer have a path to doing what they do best and have peace of mind that your service will supplement that process on their way to success.

**3. Make a list of objectives for what the customer wants to accomplish AFTER your product or service is in place.** Your objective as a professional is to get the probable purchaser to see the world as though the sale were already made.

**4. Get the customer to be a visionary.** Let him tell you what he has in mind instead of you telling him what's on yours.

**5. Make the customer commit to a future action based on their goals for achievement.** This strategy must be worded more out of conversation than sales presentation so it doesn't sound too salesy.

**5.5 Make plans for after the sale has taken place, before the sale is consummated.** Even if you don't have the commitment yet, you can try to schedule an installation time or a meeting after delivery. Assume the sale as a natural part of the conversation.

**@BAT: Start by looking at your last five sales.** How did they happen? How did you complete them? Now make a plan to incorporate those strategies into every presentation and every sales cycle.

Everyone tells you to "learn from your failures." Who the hell wants to fail? The single best lesson to learn from failure is, "DON'T DO THAT AGAIN!"

# Success is repeatable, if you learn from your past successes.

PRINCIPLE 22:

# Service is the reputation for the next sale. And the basis for a loyal customer.

**"To Serve is to Rule"**
*5,000-year-old Chinese Proverb*

**"Quality in selling starts with service."**
*John Patterson*

**"Your friendliness and willingness
to help is in direct proportion
to your success."**
*Jeffrey Gitomer*

"To serve is to rule" is a 5,000-year-old Chinese proverb. The more (and faster) people in business learn that service is the biggest part, the more their reputation will grow as an honest, ethical, helpful, and sincere business AND a businessperson worthy of repeat business and a referral.

**GREAT SERVICE CREATES REPEAT BUSINESS.** What happens between the time the first sale is made, until the next purchase is about to be made, determines who gets the next order. The "service" part of the relationship you have with your customers determines your fate for future business.

# Great service creates word-of-mouth advertising. Word-of-mouth advertising TRUMPS traditional advertising 1,000 to 1.

What's the "word" out on you?

**ALL CUSTOMERS NEED SERVICE.** The big question is: How do you respond? That response creates reputation. That reputation leads you to growth or demise. And you control it.

Why do some of your customers love you and some hate you? Why do some stay loyal and some leave? What can you do to make your service memorable? What are you doing to maintain real customer loyalty?

Loyal is the most difficult of the customer service goals to achieve. But once you have it, you have something your competition will never have – the next order. Give answers and solutions, not excuses. That's what customers want.

 **@BAT: Call five customers at random, and ask them how they feel about doing business with you.** Ask them why they would do business with you again. Then call your five best customers, and ask them why they will do business with you again. Then call five customers you lost, and find out why you lost them.

Those twenty answers, when combined and studied, will give you the answers you need to grow and prosper with a combination of new customers and well-retained old customers.

PRINCIPLE 23:

# Extra service leads to the "testimonial word."

**"Give them that little extra service which keeps customers pleased... remember, a satisfied user is the best advertisement you can have."**
*John Patterson*

**"Exceptional service breeds testimonials."**
*Jeffrey Gitomer*

All customers expect great service. Very few get it.

Your biggest job is not to sell and serve. Your biggest job is to deliver *memorable* service.

Going beyond what is expected means that you anticipate, surprise, delight, and even rescue your customer at a precise moment in time. Consistently going beyond what's expected leads to stories, referrals, and testimonials.

Facts and figures are forgotten, but stories are retold again and again. Exceptional service lowers the barrier to testimonial sales. If you have created exceptional opportunities for your customer, they will be more than happy to tell their story to the media and to other prospective customers. They will spread the word.

And their word is both truth and proof.

How are you treating your customers?
What are your customers saying about you?

 **You don't need permission from a boss to make a customer feel great.** Make one customer feel *great* today and every day. If you are the boss, do the same for your internal customers (your employees).

**THINK!** about a time when you felt good because you received great service. Make someone else feel that good.

*Here are your possibilities as you look at the service process:*

- **Your customer MAY come back if the product was good and the service was acceptable (this is satisfied).**

- **Your customer WILL come back if the product was great (this is loyal).**

- **Your customer WILL COME BACK AND TELL OTHERS if the product was the greatest, and the service was memorable (that is the definition of loyal, testimonial, and referral).**

 **@BAT: Look at your last five referrals.** How did they come about? Measure how many unsolicited referrals you get each week. Five should be a minimum number. Then create a game plan of what you can do EVERY DAY that the customer would consider memorable, and do that.

# Customer service is not about who's right or wrong. It's about how you react to, respond, and handle the problem. And how you handle the problem determines the fate of your relationship.

*— Jeffrey Gitomer*

PRINCIPLE 24:

# Referrals are better earned than asked for.

**"Satisfied users are always your best advertisement, and the more of them you have in your territory the more money you will make."**
*John Patterson*

**"A referral is the easiest sale to make."**
*Jeffrey Gitomer*

The two types of referrals are solicited and unsolicited.

A solicited referral is one that you ask for. Unsolicited referrals are the ones that you earn.

There are two basic forms of unsolicited referrals: customer-driven and word-of-mouth-driven. Unsolicited referrals are like a business report card – they will tell you how well you are performing in the marketplace. You will ONLY get an unsolicited referral when you are at the highest level of market performance and reputation.

If you have a happy customer, you can earn a referral. But earning referrals requires extra work. Service is the key. Excellent service provided by you, along with the excellent service provided by your company, is the best formula for gaining and earning referrals.

**If you make 100 cold calls, how many sales will you make?** If you get 100 referrals, how many sales will you make? Get it? The highest percentage sale is a referral.

**THE ONE-WORD DEFINITION OF REFERRAL IS RISK.** Someone is willing to risk their friendship or relationship with another to have them contact you for a purchase. People are only willing to risk when they are confident and comfortable that the risk is low and the possible rewards are so high that they outweigh any hesitancy in giving the referral.

Are you willing to refer your clients or customers to someone else? Is someone else willing to refer their clients or customers to you? Answer: Yes, if there is mutual trust.

# You could double your business if you got every one of your present customers to REFER one more customer just like themselves.

**@BAT: List your five biggest customers. Then list your five best customers (relationship-wise).** Are they the same? They better be, or you're in trouble. If not, stop here and develop a game plan to make that happen within one year. List five ways you can earn a referral. Make a game plan to implement each referral strategy.

# Advertising brings awareness. Testimonial advertising brings customers.

**"A satisfied user is the best advertisement you could have."**
*John Patterson*

**"Word-of-mouth advertising is 50 times more powerful than advertising."**
*Jeffrey Gitomer*

Everyone wants to be well known. Everyone wants to be a household word. Everyone wants to be perceived as a leader. And everyone makes the mistake of tooting their own horn in an ad. One third-party endorsement, one testimonial ad, is worth a hundred self-praising ads.

Patterson used several forms of advertising. He tried everything from sending out a circular to 5,000 prospects, to creating enticing window displays at his stores that would lure probable purchasers in.

But the most effective form of advertising he found was the use of testimonials. Once he realized that satisfied users were the best advertisement, he encouraged all his salesmen to advertise themselves by becoming identified with the people who were in a position to help them: their loyal customers.

"My registers have saved me the expense of two clerks and increased my volume about 30%."

Cleveland, Tenn.

"Approximately 24% increase in our grocery department sales. At the same time, we have been able to reduce payroll expense in this department approximately 10%."

Pittsburgh, Pa.

"Had a direct saving of $1,820.00 per year in clerk hire alone. Charge business increased immediately."

Dallas, Texas

"Could not possibly handle my present volume without it."

Indianapolis, Ind.

"This system gives us the lowest operating cost we have yet had the pleasure to enjoy."

New York City

"As a result of our change to self-service, volume in store increased more than 60%."

Burlington, Iowa

"Of all the equipment we have placed in our stores during our years of business, none has given us such a great return on our investment as these registers."

Johnson City, Tenn.

"Had I not hesitated so long to avail myself of the advantages your registers offer, I would have been many thousands of dollars better off today."

Redwood City, Calif.

"Since changing to self-service, our volume has increased with same employees, thus reducing expense percentage ... we now handle both cash and charge business with greater ease and efficiency."

Oak Park, Ill.

"After changing to self-service, our sales volume showed a large increase without increasing expenses ... we now have control over departments, cash and charge sales, and tax collections."

St. Louis, Mo.

**BEFORE**

"Self-service increased our sales over 300% first year. Kept overhead down. Profit greater than we expected it could be. We do both cash and charge business."

Spokane, Wash.

**AFTER**

*you too can enjoy similar benefits ..*

*The NCR Archive at the Montgomery Historical Society*

Testimonial ad that appeared on May 21, 1947.

# Testimonials are reputation power and sales power.

*A testimonial ad creates 5.5 winning situations:*

1. **It provides proof that your product is what you say it is.**

2. **It builds credibility and reputation.**

3. **It strengthens the loyalty bond between you and the customer in the ad.**

4. **It's the only proof you've got.**

5. **It reduces the risk of purchasing.**

5.5 **It deflates the competition (especially if it is a testimonial of a customer who switched).**

 **Who are your five best customers?** How did they choose you? Did they switch from a competitor? Do they find value in your services beyond your price? Will they do a testimonial for you?

If you can create an army of people talking about you, instead of a bunch of self-righteous drivel about "we're the greatest," you'll make more sales than you ever dreamed. The question is *do you have an army of people who love you enough to spread the word?*

 **@BAT: Create a video testimonial for every aspect of your product benefits and your selling process.** Work them into your sales presentation at the appropriate times. Watch your sales increase.

When a spokesperson or a salesperson speaks of himself, his company, or his product, he is either selling, or bragging, or both.

When a loyal customer speaks on behalf of the product in the form of a testimonial, it is proof, and, in fact, it is the only proof that a salesperson has to substantiate his claims.

# Testimonials will sell when the salesman can't.

If a customer is on the fence and is choosing between one company and another, it is the testimonial, not the salesperson, that will sway the decision.

Testimonials, like referrals, are report cards. If you are having trouble getting them, that's not a problem. That's a symptom. And you better look deeper into your method of doing business or your product's capability to find the answer.

Most salespeople mistakenly blame the customer when they can't get a referral or testimonial. Big mistake.

**"Overcome objections with testimonials."**
*John Patterson*

**"One testimonial has more strength than a hundred presentations."**
*Jeffrey Gitomer*

# Testimonials are PROOF... and they're the only proof you've got.

When is the right time to ask for a testimonial?

Not sure? That might be the reason you don't have as many as you would like. You may be asking at the wrong time or asking the wrong people.

Do you have a notebook full of testimonial letters categorized by topic? Don't throw them all out at once – replace them with video. Isn't it about time to put your testimonials into 21st-century technology? Isn't a video more powerful than a letter? And make CERTAIN that the testimonials cover any objection or barrier a potential customer may have regarding price, quality, and value.

 **@BAT: Select your five BEST customers.** The ones who really love you. Make an appointment to see them for a testimonial. A VIDEO testimonial. Make live recordings of what they think of you.

A collection of video testimonials will go further than any other sales tool or advertisement campaign times ten.

Make a video testimonial CD, and the world is your oyster. If you use just letters, you're just like every other clam.

If you only do ONE THING from this entire book, get video testimonials to support your claims and build your reputation.

I can make you one promise about testimonials, one iron-clad guarantee: THEY WORK.

*– Jeffrey Gitomer*

PRINCIPLE 26:

# Success in business is not just about people, it's about GREAT people.

**"I want to create a team of men to help carry out great ideas, not just a team of men."**
*John Patterson*

**"I often hear business owners and managers complaining that it's hard to find good people. 'There's no good people out there,' they lament. Here's the reality. There's plenty of good people out there pal, they're just not working for you."**
*Jeffrey Gitomer*

I hire eagles. I do it because I want people who have brains, a positive attitude, and a great work ethic – people who want to succeed and are eager to learn new things. With eagles, you can fly.

The challenge is that eagles are independent. And sometimes they fly away. You have to take this risk if you want a great business. You also have to reward eagles.

At the time of this writing, my eagles number 35. I treat them like the champions they are. I encourage, I teach, I lead by example, I set the work ethic by my own work standards, and I give them more than they would get elsewhere.

I pay them well. But, more than that, I give them a great place to work, plenty of health, dental, and life insurance, and a 401K plan. I even take it several steps further.

Free food and drinks, AAA memberships, YMCA health club memberships, Sam's club and COSTCO memberships, and birthday parties where lunch is catered in for everyone.

I do not consider my eagles a "team" – I prefer to call them "my family." I feel like if I treat everyone like I treat members of my family (and I do have family – my brother and daughters – working there as well), that they will feel at home at work. Family is a closer knit group than team.

I reward people for making mistakes. One hundred bucks if you screw up big. People are floored when they get it, but besides crying and feeling like dirt, they learn the lesson, and are given the money for the courage to have risked and failed. No one wants to make a mistake. And when they do, I want to make certain that they feel bad, AND good. It works.

How do you find eagles? You don't – they find you. If your business is attractive, and has a great reputation, people will call. Your job is to discern between the callers. Some eagles are disguised as hawks, vultures, and chickens.

**@BAT: Gather your eagles for a weekend retreat and ask them to discuss their common strengths.** Ask for their insight about the future of the business and what changes they would like to see implemented. Assign tasks BEFORE you go home.

PRINCIPLE 27:

# Competition means prepare to be your best.

### "Treat competition fairly."
*John Patterson*

### "Competition does not mean war. It means learn, it means prepare, and it means be your best."
*Jeffrey Gitomer*

Competitors want the business just as much as you do. They will fight, they will undercut, they will play dirty, and they will go to any length to prevent you from getting the sale. Your job is to get the sale and maintain your highest standard of doing business.

This can be accomplished by out-thinking, out-valuing, and out-performing the competition. And you have thousands of people who will help you at any moment in time. You know them – they are your own loyal customers.

*Here are 2.5 ways to address and deal with the competition:*

**1. Go "over" the competition.** The ideal way to win. It assumes that you take the high ground. It doesn't mean sit back and wait. It means rise above in such a way that the competition has to respond or lose. Here are a few "over" ways: e-zine, seminars, and referrals. Building value by building profit. Earning testimonials and using them to get "over" again.

Others speaking on your behalf is better than any sales pitch "against" someone else. I'll make you one promise: If you invest the time and effort it takes to go "over" the competition, you will be rewarded beyond your wildest dreams AND sales will be easier and more fun.

And once you reach a high level of "over," you will be qualified for the highest level …

**2. Ignore the competition.** I have spent the last ten years ignoring the competition and building my presentation skills and writing skills. Competitors read my weekly article in their hometown. They hate me, and I love it.

Do I know them? Some. Most I don't. Sales and competition share the same adage. "It's not who you know, it's who knows you." Sounds a bit stuffy, but let me assure you that it's better to build your skills than to try to "beat" someone.

# I go for "best," not "beat." It's a better, cleaner win.

Do I always win? No. But I always feel I should have. And I have a self-confidence that keeps me ready for the next opportunity. I wake up the next day and go to work sharpening my skills.

My ways of dealing with my competition (over or ignore) are the hardest ways – but they work. And the longer you go "over" them, the more you can ignore them.

Yes, I want to beat the crap out of the competition – it's instinctive. But a smarter path is to have them looking over their shoulders to see where you are.

# Let them "hear your footsteps" and beat them by being "chosen" or "preferred."

**2.5 DO NOT TRY TO UNDER-BID or UNDER-PRICE THEM.** With rare exception (Southwest Airlines being one of them), the guy with the lowest price is also the guy with the least value and the least profit.

*Here are some* **THINK!** *questions:*

> **How many ways are there to deal with the competition?**
>
> **How do you deal with them?**
>
> **What do you say about them?**
>
> **How do you beat them?**
>
> **How often do you beat them?**

The goal is to separate yourself from the competition and from everyone else.

 **Have creative, new ideas.** Have what you're selling in finished form (design done, preliminary layout, sample). Have a WOW! multimedia presentation. Have a comparison chart of key areas where you beat the competition. Got boring business cards? Get new ones made, even if it's money out of your own pocket.

**IMPORTANT NOTE:** Don't down the competition. If you have nothing nice to say, say nothing. This is a tempting rule to break. The sirens are sweetly singing. Set yourself apart from them with preparation and creativity. Don't slam them. Downing the competition is not a no-win situation; it's an absolute losing situation.

When a prospect picks you over the competition, it's a day to celebrate – and a day to discover "why." When you figure out why you were chosen, all you have to do is repeat the process.

It's the same when you lose. Figure out why.

**@BAT: Look at your last five sales where you were chosen over the competition.** Write down the primary factors of why you won. Do the same thing for losses. Look at your last five sales that you LOST to the competition. Write down the primary factors of WHY you lost.

Now all you have to do is strengthen the reasons why you were chosen and improve the reasons you weren't. PRESTO! More sales – and you can thank the competition for helping you win them.

**Free GitBit**...**Odds are, you were chosen because the customer felt your product was better or your relationship was better.** If you would like 4.5 reasons that customers will choose you over the competition, go to www.gitomer.com, register if you're a first-time visitor, and enter the words BEAT COMPETITION in the GitBit box.

PRINCIPLE 28:

# Recognize and thank those who have helped you succeed.

**"People seldom improve themselves when they have no other model but themselves to look after."**
*John Patterson*

**"When you reward achievement, you set the stage for more achievement."**
*Jeffrey Gitomer*

Don't forget to say thank you to those who have helped you along the way. This is true not only if you are a salesperson, this is true for the corporate executives who still have their own washroom and private cafeteria.

Patterson did a tremendous job thanking not only his sales team but *all* of his employees. From rewards through the still-existing "100 Point Club," to factory improvements and incentives, Patterson did his best to reward and satisfy each person's need for appreciation.

You don't become a success on your own. And it doesn't happen overnight. You may even be lucky enough to have a mentor or two. Be smart enough to thank them.

Take the time to acknowledge the people who have helped you succeed. Learn to thank them all.

You need coworkers to help you succeed at all different levels of career achievement. The boss can help you, and so can the truck driver. And most of the time, the lower-level people provide the most help. Acknowledge them. Thank them. Reward them. Let them know you care. Let them know you are grateful for their help.

**NOTICE:** You will always see the words "Thank You!" on each and every receipt you are given. Patterson started that.

 **@BAT: List the five people you want to thank and acknowledge.** Get a small gift of remembrance for them. I give autographed books. Go to www.executivebooks.com and buy the set of books by Charlie "Tremendous" Jones. If you request autographed copies, he will sign them all for no additional cost. I keep a dozen on hand for gifts – and people love them.

# Oh, and THANK YOU for being my customer.

**THINK!** about positively impacting others in the same way you have been impacted. Having a mentor is a gift and can make a world of difference to the person you've invested in. Pass it on.

PRINCIPLE 29:

# To get loyalty, you must GIVE loyalty.

**"If it's only money you get out of your job, you don't get enough."**
*John Patterson*

**"Customer loyalty is the highest level of business achievement."**
*Jeffrey Gitomer*

Patterson wrote, "Believe in your goods. Be loyal to your company. Put your heart in your work." He wrote those words in 1889. He espoused the principles of loyalty without actually saying the word.

*The four pillars of loyalty that I practice and preach are:*

I.   **Loyalty to your company**

II.  **Loyalty to your product**

III. **Loyalty to your customer**

IV.  **Loyalty to yourself**

Combine Patterson's words with my four pillars of loyalty and you will discover the foundation for building long-term business success.

So, how do you get to "loyal" in the relationships with your customers? Simple – apply the principles that build loyalty in every other aspect of your life.

Well, sort of simple.

*My criteria to determine loyalty is:*

> **1. Will the customer do business with me again?**
>
> **2. Will the customer proactively refer me to other probable purchasers?**

*My philosophy about loyalty is:*

> **If I am loyal to my customers, they will be loyal to me.**
>
> **If I refer other customers to my customers, I am giving them my loyalty, thereby earning theirs.**
>
> **If I set the example by doing for my customers what I want done to me, I will receive what I want by virtue of earning it rather than expecting it or asking for it. Earning is the most powerful way of gaining anything.**

The easiest loyalty lessons are the ones you learn at home, either by positive or negative example.

Foundations of all buildings and houses start with pillars. Without the proper foundation, you have an unstable building and an unstable customer.

It is the same in business. If you don't have the four pillars of loyalty, your business foundation is shaky.

You must have loyalty to all four pillars.

**Loyalty is the highest mark.**

**Loyalty is success.**

**Loyalty is solid gold.**

**Loyalty is golden business.**

**Loyalty is unyielding, unrelenting, and every faithful. True to the end.**

**Loyalty is your golden opportunity to ring your register by earning it from others.**

"The best way to get loyalty is to earn it."

*Jeffrey Gitomer*

# Loyalty is more delicate with customers because there is a balance of money and value. And loyalty is not just granted – it's an earned distinction.

*– Jeffrey Gitomer*

# Decide. It doesn't matter if it's right or wrong. Decide!

**"An executive is a man who decides. Sometimes he decides right. But he always decides."**
*John Patterson*

**"If you want to succeed, you have to fail a few times."**
*Max Gitomer*
*(my father)*

Making a decision involves risk and courage.

This was Patterson's way of saying "Take a risk, take a chance." His whole life was risk and chance. He often made decisions that risked his last dime.

**INSIGHT:** Patterson didn't take risks. He took calculated risks.

Patterson was a decision maker. And he demanded the same from his executives. He could tolerate employees who made mistakes, but had no patience with people who feared or hesitated to make a decision.

Decision making came quite easy to Patterson for the simple fact that he had the instinctive and inveterate habit of analyzing situations realistically instead of nominally.

Patterson would reach a decision, no matter how important or menial, by using his famous pyramid chart. He even went as far as standardizing this chart for the people on his team.

The objective needing to be reached (the decision) would be at the apex of the pyramid. Then he added a realistic analysis of the means by which the objective might be attained.

He standardized this method of decision-making throughout the organization so it became habitual for all employees in the company to use when a decision needed to be reached.

Patterson wanted all his people to think alike, or at least like him. The pyramid chart was the visual symbol of this.

**THINK!** about the last few decisions you delayed. Why did you? Uncertainty? Timing not "right?" Not wanting to take the risk? Afraid of repercussions? You can always change the direction you are going, but not if you are standing still.

Postponing a decision comes from lack of information. And postponing a decision comes from a lack of factual information to make a sound judgment. Postponing a decision comes from confusion or disorganization. Postponing a decision comes from doubt or fear.

## It's not a matter of 'can't' decide. It's a matter of 'won't' decide. Can't means won't.

**NOTE:** Monday-morning quarterbacks are the best non-decision makers in the world. They look at someone who took a risk, decided incorrectly, and now here they come saying, "Well, that's not what I would have done!" as they sit with their beer on their chicken's nest, yelling at the TV.

## How do you come to decisions? Is it systematic? Or feeling?

## Can't make decisions? Try to use Patterson's way: the Pyramid Chart.

This pyramid chart was drawn by Patterson on the back page of a book on longevity. Patterson was inspired by reading and took immediate action to write down ideas, concepts, and thoughts.

**@BAT: Make a pyramid chart for yourself.** Start with a decision you'll have to make soon. Refer to the Patterson definitions and examples. Often when you write out the possibilities, the right decision becomes obvious.

**Free Git✗Bit**...**Want more information on making decisions – why people decide and what prevents decisions from being made?** Go to www.gitomer.com, register if you're a first-time visitor, and enter the word DECISION in the GitBit box.

Pyramid chart in the hand of John Patterson.

# You become known by the actions you take. Take ethical actions.

**"There was a time when all successful salesmen were liars. That time has passed."**
*John Patterson*

**"You are more known and judged for your deeds and your actions than for your words."**
*Jeffrey Gitomer*

What is ethical? Who decides?

*Use the 5.5 question acid test during the presentation:*

1.   Is this in the best long-term interest of the customer?
2.   Is this in the best long-term interest of my company?
3.   Is this in the best long-term interest of my career?
4.   If I were the probable purchaser, would I buy?
5.   Is it something that would make my mother proud?
5.5  Am I telling the truth?

These 5.5 questions are at the heart of ethics in the selling process, and the heart of ethics in any business. They must be asked every time a business interaction takes place and every time a sale is being proposed.

Patterson knew 100 years ago the importance of ethics in business and wanted his people to portray a trusting, pleasing, and earnest image.

# My experience has shown me that if you have to say what you are, you probably aren't.

**THINK!** about that for a moment. "I'm honest," "I'm ethical," even "I'm the decision-maker," "I'm the boss," or "I'm in charge," usually indicates just the opposite. Doesn't it?

*There are easy ways to measure the results of your ethics:*

- **Can you sell the same customer again?**

- **Has the customer referred you another customer – without being asked to do so?** Get proof of your ethics, get better, or get out.

- **Remember the movie "Pinocchio"?** And Jiminy Cricket on the shoulder of Pinocchio? His thought-provoking song, "Always Let Your Conscience Be Your Guide," (and you can probably sing the chorus right now) was a statement of shunning bad ethics. Didn't you already know what he was going to say? And don't you already know what to do? You don't need to ask yourself about ethics. You simply need to take ethical actions from what you already know. If you have any questions, call your mother.

# If you have done your homework and prepared well, it will be evident in your success report card.

*"Remember, the demonstration has but one object, the sale of the register. No matter how well you think you have demonstrated the register, if you do not close the sale, you have failed in your purpose."*
*John Patterson*

*"Weak salespeople look at quotas and become fearful. Mediocre salespeople look at quotas as a goal. Great salespeople look at quotas and laugh."*
*Jeffrey Gitomer*

Patterson established the first quota system used. When he established the system, it was a relative number based on the salesman's territory. It was a reflection of what the salesman should be able to bring in based upon the wealth of his territory. Back then, and still today, quotas were a system to measure the minimum standard of achievement.

If you were a Boy Scout, your motto was "Be Prepared." Your dad and mom drubbed into you your whole life, "Do your homework!" This was not an exercise. It was a lesson. Doing your homework never ends. You did it in school. Now you must do it in business, or lose to someone who does.

*Here's my rule called "The Rule of The More, The More":*

- **The more you believe, the more you will sell.**

- **The more value you provide to others, the more people will come to know and respect you.**

- **The more you study business, the more you will know how to react to any business situation.**

- **The more you study sales, the more you will know how to react to any sales situation.**

## Reach GOALS, not quotas. Think being BEST, not quotas, and goals just show up.

Max Gitomer, my dad, always went into a sales call with a yellow legal pad full of homework and almost always left with a deal, or the sale. I wonder if there's a correlation. Homework by definition is "work" that you do at "home." That means turn off the TV and turn on your computer. That means turn off the TV and turn on the Internet. That means reading instead of watching. That means thinking instead of drinking. That means preparing, which will lead to winning.

If you prepare well, and execute the fundamentals to the BEST of your ability, goals will get met, and quotas will get blown away.

**THINK!** about what is keeping you from reaching your goals and being your best.

PRINCIPLE 32.5:

# If it has been working for 100 years or more, don't even think about changing it.

*"There is nothing new under the sun but there are lots of old things we don't know."*
*Ambrose Bierce*

*"If you want to learn something new or get a new idea, read a book that's 70 years old."*
*Jeffrey Gitomer*

Tradition is everywhere. Football rivalries that date back over 100 years. Religious ceremonies. Democrats versus Republicans. Holidays and parades.

People are attracted to, and attracted by, tradition. They fly thousands of miles and stand in huge crowds in the freezing cold to participate. They talk about it. They compare it to last year or years gone by.

The principles, strategies, and ideas that I am presenting to you are no different.

The reason things have been around for 100 years is that they have been working for 100 years. Family traditions like Thanksgiving dinner, or the Italian seven-fish dinner on Christmas Eve, etiquette traditions like thanking people and welcoming people (without the use of a computer), and personal financial traditions like saving or investing a percentage of your income.

They are so traditional that they are irrefutable.

If you can identify the traditions of your business and become a master at them, you will not only be successful, you will also be respected.

# Tradition is a sacred, powerful insurance of success.

**PATTERSON'S TRADITION OF THE 100 POINT CLUB.** Patterson was the first businessman to offer incentives and rewards to employees. The 100 Point Club was started for salesman in the NCR American Selling Force who sold over 100 points per month any time after January 1, 1906. (Each register was appointed a specific point value.)

The insignia of this exclusive club is a solitaire diamond mounted on a solid gold star, the star being emblematic of the high standard of salesmanship and the gem of the quality of his ability. This club still meets nearly 100 years later. That's tradition.

The benefit to the winners was an all-expense paid, two-week convention in Ohio with the officers of the company. Patterson started dangling hefty rewards for those who exceeded their sales goals. Some rewards were as large and grand as a new car. Each and every reward was carefully calculated to grasp the desire of the salesman. Only merchandise of the highest quality was given.

*The NCR Archive at the Montgomery Historical Society*

CPC convention, 1920.
John Patterson front row, second from right.

All NCR salesmen were working for something beyond salary and commission. They had something extra to strive for. And in turn, the incentives and rewards produced hard-working, goal-achieving, and dedicated salesmen. Those incentives are still working for men and women all over the world.

"Loyalty Produces Leaders" was the motto adopted by the members of the 100 Point Club during their first annual convention. This motto explains how the men who attended the convention gained the high honor of being the leaders of the American selling force.

The 100 Pointers are loyal:

1. **To their company**
2. **To their company's methods**
3. **To their own ideas of high-class salesmanship**
4. **To excellent and ethical business practices**
5. **To themselves**

The 100 Point Club was a celebration, an acknowledgment, and a learning experience. I have had the privilege and the honor of addressing that group at their convention. It was a thrill and a challenge.

Traditions are a valuable asset and a link to success. They link the past with the present. They help you see what has been done. They help you remember what to do. And they give you the confidence that you can do it again because it's been done before.

# Traditions are there for you to learn from and embrace.

# They are there to help you succeed.

# Reward those who have helped you succeed with a public display of appreciation.
### – John Patterson

# "Tradition!"
## Sung by Tevye the milkman in "Fiddler on the Roof"

# People will try to rain on your parade because they have no parade of their own.
### – Jeffrey Gitomer

**TRADITIONS OF SUCCESS AND PRINCIPLES FOR LIFE.** If you are a 120-year-old company, you've got tradition. Lots of it. There are things you have kept and enhanced over the years. Two big ones at NCR are *The Primer* and the 100 Point Club.

# Some traditions get eliminated that, in retrospect, you realize or wish you had kept.

If you're NOT a 120-year-old company, pay attention. The old ones got there on a different set of values and principles than you or I did. And they had to watch the world make radical changes every decade, and adapt to them or die.

NCR had a magazine called *The Hustler.* (See inset at right.) It started in 1884 and for some reason was eliminated.

*The NCR Archive at the Montgomery Historical Society*
**The Hustler** magazine

Its purpose was to communicate ideas, news, and the successes of NCR. These days, when people think of *Hustler* magazine, a more risqué offering comes to mind. But in its day, *The Hustler* depicted what Patterson wanted the salesperson to do: hustle.

Part of succeeding is moving quickly (hustling), and in those days it was all about getting from one place to the next as fast as they could. At the turn of the last century, they couldn't hop in a car and get to the next place. There were no cars in 1889. They had to catch the train to get to the next city.

A favorite item in my library is called, *The Fuller Bristler*. It's one year's worth of the Fuller Brush Company weekly newsletters, written by their own (door-to-door) salesmen. The salesmen referred to themselves as "pluggers." The first issue that year (1925) was a bunch of thoughts that were inspired by "pluggers." It was a way that salesmen (they had no women either) could help each other.

They didn't have cell phones or e-mails back then to communicate. The newsletter was the only way they could connect and communicate about sales techniques and ideas. It was about one salesperson sharing information and encouraging another salesperson.

That's the way it was in 1925. That's the way it's supposed to be. And that's the way it is in successful businesses and organizations today.

It was no different at NCR. Magazines and newsletters were a traditional part of their person-to-person support.

But NCR went much further. Patterson's brilliance was that he would bring his executives, managers, and salespeople together for a conference. He would make all of them show up and dress up. Subliminally he was saying, "All my guys look alike; therefore, they share the same problems." His brilliance was in his subtleties.

He taught them, he challenged them, he let them interface with each other, he communicated with them weekly, and he rewarded them for their success. In public.

And when you repeat that process year after year, it becomes tradition. A tradition of successfully repeated actions, deeds, and principles. You have won in the past, there's no reason you won't win today. And tomorrow. In other words: You win because you believe you will win and that you personally are a winner.

**THE POWER OF A FLIPCHART.** Is the flipchart a tradition? John Patterson used one in 1900, and, despite all the technological advances, I still use one more than 100 years later. It's still the best communication and idea-clarification medium I know. I bought my first one in 1972. (That's me on the right.)

1972 was a breakthrough year for me. I was learning the science of selling. I was under-funded (OK, almost broke). And it's the year I got attitude.

The flipchart played an integral part in my decision-making and my attitude achievement that year, but I didn't realize the power of it until 30 years later. All I did was put a bunch of things on the flipchart that told me what I had to do in order to attain a positive attitude, and I kept the flipchart open to the page until I did it.

Part of my training regimen was reading one chapter of Napoleon Hill's book each day. The book only has 15 chapters. And part of it was making sure I lived the attitude each day, even though my life was not in the best condition at the time. (Ever been in that situation?) The twins were just born, I was in a rotten marriage, and I was broke.

Flipchart – Patterson (left) and Gitomer.

But when people came up to me and asked me how it was going, I would say, "GREAT!" (even though it was pretty crappy).

I've saved about 50 flipchart pads over the years. I save everything. Including my positive attitude. I know where to find it. It's always with me. I'm always wearing it. And it will be with me until the last minute of the last day.

I use a flipchart at the beginning of an idea or the beginning of a project. I use it to get ready to write each book. I use it to market each book.

The flipchart can define and outline ideas and concepts in a way that creates detail you hadn't thought of. As you write each point, it sort of spurs your mind to the next point, and makes you say, "Oh, yeah" while you write furiously.

Sometimes I copy the sheet on my laptop. Sometimes I tape several of the sheets on the wall as I brainstorm, but since I have already written it down, it's also subliminally in "the force" area in the back of my head.

# I execute each of the ideas through osmosis. I already have it down on paper. That's the beginning of mental clarification and physical action.

I am not good at detailed planning. But I'm good at thinking. I'm good at writing. And I am good at creating. The flipchart is the perfect medium for all three of those.

It's big. It's blank. And it's conducive to a thoughtful, creative person. I have even gotten to the point where I'm picky about the kind of markers I use on a flipchart.

# The flipchart clarifies thinking – it extends thought – and once you have written something down, the flipchart also communicates ideas and concepts.

In many of my seminars, I use a flipchart (even though I also have a PowerPoint presentation). I love taking the flipchart, drawing a line down the middle, and asking the audience to yell out the biggest objections they get. "Price," "satisfied with present supplier," "takes the lowest bid," "won't return my calls," they scream. Same objections every time. A thousand seminars. Always the same.

Then on the other side of the sheet, I say, "Your product aside, tell me what your customer is trying to accomplish in his or her business." And they yell out, "make more sales," "keep customers loyal," "have greater productivity," "make profit." Same answers every time. A thousand seminars. Always the same answers.

Then I say, "If you could make all things on the right – the things the customer wants – come true, would your objections matter anymore? Would price matter anymore? The entire audience says the objections would fade away. The flipchart becomes this big, huge AHA! by taking something that everyone already knows, and structuring it in a way that people see it AND perceive it to be true.

Flipcharts are cheap. They cost between $50 and $200. And some of you are wondering if the boss will buy you one. MAJOR CLUE: You have your own money now. And you can begin to invest it in the most important person in the world – You.

What's one idea worth? What's an idea that you capture worth? How many ideas have you ever had that you lost because you didn't write them down? The flipchart captures, communicates, expands, and solidifies plans. And the flipchart preserves so that you can go back and see what you did and revise your plans.

## The flipchart is not an option. It's an asset. And the perfect medium to make a concept transferable.

**THE LEGEND OF THE 1904 WORLD'S FAIR.** NCR had an exhibit at the 1904 World's Fair. John Patterson was shrewd enough to convince every concessionaire to purchase a cash register and issue receipts for purchases. This ensured Patterson ultimate exposure for his machines throughout the fair.

Every exhibitor was emphatic about visitors not touching their wares. "Do not touch" signs were everywhere – except at the NCR exhibit. Patterson invited everyone to "touch." He encouraged people to try the machines and print receipts for themselves.

*The NCR Archive at the Montgomery Historical Society*

NCR exhibit at the 1904 World's Fair in St. Louis.

These actions are more proof of Patterson's winning business strategies. He did what everyone else was afraid to do.

While everyone else in the world was in the chicken coop, guarding their precious toys, Patterson was making scrambled eggs and letting everyone have a free breakfast.

What are you doing, or what have you done that completely bucked the system and worked? I'm not saying "do the opposite of everybody else." I am saying "go out on a limb" "take a risk" and "dare to use your innovative thinking because that's where the growth is, that's where the rewards are". Dare to be different, and you will dare to be great.

**THE LEGEND OF 5 AND .5.** If you ever get a chance to read *The Primer*, you will see that every time John Patterson made a point or created a rule, he would attach five points to drive it home.

The transferability (in Patterson's case, the memorization process) of each of his points corresponded to fingers on your hand. And in many cases, you would actually see an illustration of a hand and each example above a finger. A simple yet powerful technique.

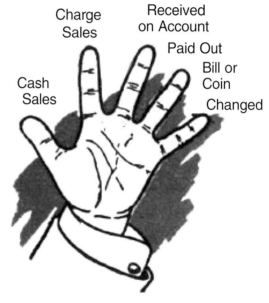

**Hand from the 1919 Primer.**

Sales folklore says that he liked the number five not just because it corresponded with fingers, but also because there were five types of money, there were five things customers would do when they walked into a store, and there were five things he wanted his salesmen to do before they walked into an appointment.

Patterson realized that business and selling was a science. He experimented, as any good scientist would, until he found formulas that worked. Then he repeated them.

And he got hundreds of his employees, executives, managers, and salespeople to repeat them.

# It was the simplicity combined with the science that made the concepts transferable and successful.

In 1992, I was hired by another speaker to help him with marketing a new program on leadership. He was already an expert on time management and had established himself with hundreds of customers.

My job was to create an additional learning program so he could go back to loyal customers who loved him and get more business.

I came up with a cool idea. I wrote the speech on leadership with eight points: Maintain a positive attitude, embrace change, deploy courage, take a risk, listen with the intent to understand, communicate to be understood, delegate and empower, understand yourself and your situation.

I explained to him that these were simple and powerful leadership qualities but that there was no "glue." So I said, "Let's do 8.5, and make the .5 'commitment' because without commitment none of the other qualities will really make you a leader."

I thought it was brilliant. But fortunately my client said, "I don't like it." "No problem," I said. "Do you mind if I use it myself?"

# And from that moment on, every list I made (or ever will make) ended with the "glue" of .5.

It has not only become a trademark, it has also become my most thought-provoking challenge. Each time I make a list, I make certain that the person who reads the list knows how to take the strategies and apply them to himself or herself by adding a .5 at the end of it.

# What's the difference between 5 and .5? Why are they even relevant to this discussion? The answer is one word: transferability.

In order for you to read, understand, incorporate, and succeed from these principles, you have to both get it AND do it. And I promise that if you get it and do it, you will also achieve the .5 – bank it.

– Jeffrey Gitomer

# The Untapped Power of the Probable Purchaser

**HERE'S THE CHALLENGE:** You've been referring to your prospective customer as a prospect for 20 years. Maybe some of you only two years.

Wrong thought. Or at least, incomplete thought, and non-inspirational thought. In your mind, you must begin the transition from thinking "prospect" to thinking "probable purchaser." It puts your mind on YES! before you start.

I'm an expert in selling. I believe myself to be the best at sales and the selling process in the world. I love the pitch, the presentation, the meeting, and all the challenge that goes with making a sale. I love when a CEO who I'm presenting to gets up and walks around, and I go sit in his chair. I love when I can convince him to say the words, "My people need to have this." Or, "My people need to see this."

## You know what that means? The register rings. Money.

I have studied the history of sales for 35 years. Every time I read something, I learn something.

# I especially love reading books more than 50 years old because old ideas are usually new ideas revised or in disguise.

When I began to study John Patterson, it changed many things about the way I thought sales should be conducted. And when I came across the words that Patterson used to define prospect, I believed it to be one of the five biggest AHA! events of my life. Not only was it brilliant, it was brilliant AND obvious.

He referred to the prospect as a *probable purchaser*. WOW!

I thought to myself, "Why doesn't everyone do that?" Some salespeople call them suspects, prospects, rejects, or defects. They call them tire kickers, price shoppers, just-lookers, and worse. They're crazy. They're already setting a negative tone in their mind for what they think will happen. The reality is they're not thinking – they're pre-judging. And there is no worse error anyone in business can commit.

Patterson, in his brilliance, set a positive tone for every potential customer that a salesperson would encounter by referring to them as a "probable purchaser." And as I've confessed, nothing that I have ever seen in the realm of business or selling has even come close to that brilliance.

If you begin now to refer to your potential customer as a "probable purchaser," it will change your entire mental outlook as you enter the meeting, try for the sale, while you make the sale, and when the sale is completed.

> # Once you have it in your mind, you will call your prospects *probable purchasers* forever because it holds your key to self-belief and self-assurance.

Your self-belief is half of your sales. It's the part that you can most easily transfer to another person. They catch your passion, your enthusiasm, and your attitude. All of that comes from self-belief. Self-belief comes from your inner thoughts and your inner language. Using the term probable purchaser will not just lead you to more sales, it will lead you to a better life. I promise.

If you think of a prospect as a prospect, you are doomed to the attitude of "maybe." If you think of them as a probable purchaser, you will walk into a sales call thinking, **"Cha-Ching!"**

# How to live the Cha-Ching! Principles

It's easy to read the principles and easy to commit them to memory. It's easy to read the principles and say to yourself, "Yeah, I already know that." But there's a big difference between KNOWING and DOING.

"Knowing" isn't living these principles. "Doing" leads to mastery. To live the principles is to incorporate them into your daily life and strive to master them. They worked 100 years ago, and they still work today.

**NOTE:** Patterson was not distracted by a TV. Neither am I. Rather, he was distracted by family and books. So am I. To understand this model of success, it may be necessary to avoid or ignore the television for some period of time. I did, and it works.

By taking action after each principle, you are learning to live the principle. However, you can't just do them, you must master them. Master the actions, and you will then live the principles to their fullest. It will take some time, and a great deal of self-discipline to even become proficient (the stepping stone to mastery), but the end result will be profitable in more ways than you can imagine. Not just in sales, not just in business, not just in career. In life.

Please also note that I didn't say "do" the principles, I said "live" them. Exercise is combining "knowing" and "doing."

**HERE'S THE FORMULA:** Knowing + Doing = Living. It's so much more powerful when they are ingrained.

*Here are 5.5 simple steps to "live" the principles:*

**1. Read.** Read to understand. Many people read to "confirm." They (not you, of course) read and think or say, "I know that." Knowing is NOTHING. It's asking yourself, "How good am I at that?" that leads to a real understanding of the principle. Reading to understand is a deeper and more powerful read.

**2. Think!** Think about how each principle translates to your career and your life. Think about how you could be more successful if you mastered each principle. Think about what it will take for you to do that. Devote 15 minutes a day to thinking, and your achievement will double.

**3. Rate Yourself.** Assess your present skill level for each principle. Mark the page at the top of each principle with a number between one and ten. That's your present reality, and you know where to go from there.

**4. Plan Yourself.** Let's say you rated yourself a six at principle number ten, Prospect for Probable Purchasers. What's your plan to raise your level of mastery to a nine at that principle? Make that plan, and put a deadline to start and a deadline to achieve – and work your butt off in the middle.

**5. Start Small, but START.** Select two principles that you have almost mastered. Figure out a way to improve on what you already have a high level of skill. Then select two principles where you are not too good, and figure out a game plan to get better at those. Most people are not good at what they don't enjoy. Your game plan to improve weaknesses should include how to have more fun in your weak areas. "Fun" leads to improvement faster than "lessons."

**5.5 Decide to Dedicate Yourself to the Self-Discipline to Succeed.** All of this information is useless to the individual who reads it and does not act. The decision to act and the dedication to follow through are the secrets. They don't sound like secrets. In fact, they sound obvious. Therein lies the flaw and the opportunity. Most people are looking for the easy way. They're the ones that buy lottery tickets, hoping to win. Those people will be looking, and losing, forever. You have an opportunity to pass all of those people, and most of the rest. All you have to do is decide to do so, and dedicate yourself to doing it.

Most people will not do the hard work it takes to make success easy.

Don't be like most people.

Put your heart into your business.
Put your heart into your job.
Put your heart into your career.

"You can not expect to be a success unless you believe whole heartedly in the value of your product and your process. You interest people, first, by the things you talk about; and, second, by the way you talk. Your talk will not ring true, your words will not carry conviction, unless you are thoroughly sold on the merit of your proposition. Believe in your goods. Be loyal to your company. Put your heart in your work."

*— Excerpt from The Primer, 1923*

# A Walk in the Graveyard

Amanda and I were going to a barbeque place for dinner.
We had arrived in Dayton to do Patterson research for
the book at the historical society. The restaurant had
a 20-minute wait. I decided to take a walk around the
neighborhood.

Three blocks later, we came to an old building that looked
like a castle split in half with a gate in the middle. "It's
a graveyard," I said. "Let's go check it out." I know this
sounds goofy, but it was a beautiful place.

The weather cooperated. Cloudy on the verge of a storm.
Dusk. Real cemetery weather. There was a car at the gate.
Security at a graveyard? Everyone's already dead. I asked
the guard if we could enter. "We're about to close, you'll
have to exit on the other side of the Welcome Center."

"No problem," I assured him. "Anyone famous buried
here?" "The Wright Brothers," he bragged. "Cool," I said.
"Anyone else?" "Here's a map," he offered. "Is John
Patterson buried here?" I asked. "Sure is. He's in area nine
at the Patterson knoll." He pointed.

I grabbed the map and searched. Found it. As we started
walking, it began to drizzle. The only thing missing was
a vampire. Giant trees made it light and dark at the same
time. It was a huge undulating park with thousands of
grave markers. Some as ornate as I've ever seen. Some 50
feet tall.

We found dates back to the early 1800s.

"Over here!" I yelled as I spotted what I thought was the Patterson gravesite. A huge marble arch marked the spot for the Patterson family. About a hundred names on it. On one wall was a brief bio of John, but I couldn't find his actual stone. Every Patterson family member had the same headstone. Smaller than a ten-pound sack of sugar. "Found it!" I screamed. Suddenly I went silent. I just stood on his grave imagining what he was like.

And then a flood of emotion came over me as I imagined the struggle, the risk, the creativity, the pioneering, the leadership, the setbacks, the victory, and every conceivable episode of business life when ultimate success occurs. The vision.

One hundred and eighteen years after his NCR adventure began, as I stood on the grave of John Patterson, an energy ran through my body that told me I was meant to be there. Ever get a feeling like that? Powerful and frightening at the same time.

I was inspired. I was energized. I was ready to take on this century-old task as though I was chosen for it.

Rain was falling as we left. "Pretty cool, huh?" I meekly offered to Amanda. "Unreal. What were the chances of this happening?" she said. "I wonder if it was a long shot or a predetermined one?"

Looking at the sky and the skyline, I said, "Serendipity, I've been told, is God's way of remaining anonymous."

I have chosen, and I have been chosen, to share this information, to take the principles, philosophies, and strategies of John Patterson, and memorialize them for the 21st century.

As you read them, I'm sure you found as I did that they are as (or more) valid today as they were then. All you have to do now is adapt them to your business and put them into practice.

**JEFFREY GITOMER**
Chief Executive Salesman

# Take them for yourself.

# Take them for your business.

# Take them for your sales.

# Take them for your success.

# Take them to the bank.

# The Cha-Ching! Principles of Business Success

1. Think!

2. Self-belief. The most convincing characteristic of a person.

3. Positive mental attitude is determined by you. Not others.

4. Boot camp separates the winner from the wanna-be winner.

5. Survival and success are a combination of knowing and doing.

6. Studying. The first discipline of knowledge.

7. Your library is the artesian well of knowledge.

8. Planning prevents wandering and provides direction.

9. Use "today time management."

10. Prospect for probable purchasers to build your business organically.

11. Increase business connections to increase sales.

12. Creating the demand converts selling to buying.

13. A prepared demonstration means personalized.

14. Gain interest with information about the customer– not your company, your product, or you.

15. Questions lead to answers. Answers lead to harmony. Answers lead to productivity. Answers lead to customers.

16. Listening leads to understanding.

17. Less sell-talk-time lead to more-buy-time.

18. Your message must be as compelling as your product to engage anyone – especially your customer.

19. An objection is the gateway to a sale.

20. Selling is not manipulating; selling is harmonizing.

21. Complete the sale with an agreement to buy and be certain to give them a receipt.

22. Service is the reputation for the next sale. And the basis for a loyal customer.

23. Extra service leads to the "testimonial word."

24. Referrals are better earned than asked for.

25. Advertising brings awareness. Testimonial advertising brings customers.

26. Success in business is not just about people, it's about GREAT people.

27. Competition means prepare to be your best.

28. Recognize and thank those who have helped you succeed.

29. To get loyalty, you must GIVE loyalty.

30. Decide. It doesn't matter if it's right or wrong. Decide!

31. You become known by the actions you take. Take ethical actions.

32. If you have done your homework and prepared well, it will be evident in your success report card.

32.5 If it has been working for 100 years or more, don't even think about changing it.

*Jeffrey Gitomer*
*Chief Executive Salesman*

**AUTHOR.** Jeffrey Gitomer is the author of *The New York Times* best-sellers *The Sales Bible, The Little Red Book of Selling, The Little Red Book of Sales Answers, The Little Black Book of Connections, The Little Gold Book of YES! Attitude* and *The Little Green Book of Getting Your Way.* All of his books have been number-one best-sellers on Amazon.com including *Customer Satisfaction is Worthless, Customer Loyalty is Priceless,* and *The Patterson Principles of Selling.* Jeffrey's books have sold more than a million copies worldwide.

**OVER 100 PRESENTATIONS A YEAR.** Jeffrey gives public and corporate seminars, runs annual sales meetings, and conducts live and Internet training programs on selling and customer loyalty. He has presented an average of 120 seminars a year for the past 15 years.

**IN FRONT OF MILLIONS OF READERS EVERY WEEK.** Jeffrey's syndicated column, *Sales Moves*, appears in business publications worldwide and is read by more than 4 million people every week.

**SALES CAFFEINE.** Jeffrey's weekly e-zine, *Sales Caffeine,* is a sales wake-up call delivered every Tuesday morning to more than 250,000 subscribers, free of charge. *Sales Caffeine* allows Jeffrey to communicate valuable sales information, strategies, and answers to sales professionals on a timely basis. To subscribe, click on FREE EZINE at www.gitomer.com.

**ON THE INTERNET.** Jeffrey's WOW! Web sites, www.gitomer.com and www.trainone.com, get as many as 25,000 hits a day from readers and seminar attendees. His state-of-the-art Web presence and e-commerce ability has set the standard among peers, and has won huge praise and acceptance from customers.

**TRAINONE ONLINE SALES TRAINING.** Online sales training lessons are available at www.trainone.com. The content is pure Jeffrey – fun, pragmatic, real world, and immediately implementable. TrainOne's innovation is leading the way in the field of customized e-learning.

**SELLING POWER LIVE.** Jeffrey is the host and commentator of *Selling Power Live,* a monthly, subscription-based sales resource bringing together the insights of the world's foremost authorities on selling and personal development.

**SALES ASSESSMENT ONLINE.** The world's first customized sales assessment, renamed a "successment," will not only judge your selling skill level in 12 critical areas of sales knowledge, but it will also give you a diagnostic report that includes 50 mini sales lessons. This amazing sales tool will rate your sales abilities and explain your customized opportunities for sales knowledge growth. This program is aptly named KnowSuccess because *you can't know success until you know yourself.*

**AWARD FOR PRESENTATION EXCELLENCE.** In 1997, Jeffrey was awarded the designation of Certified Speaking Professional (CSP) by the National Speakers Association. The CSP award has been given less than 500 times in the past 25 years and is the association's highest earned award.

**BIG CORPORATE CUSTOMERS.** Jeffrey's customers include Coca-Cola, D.R. Horton, Caterpillar, BMW, BNC Mortgage, MacGregor Golf, Ferguson Enterprises, Kimpton Hotels, Hilton, Enterprise Rent-A-Car, AmeriPride, NCR, Stewart Title, Comcast Cable, Time Warner Cable, Liberty Mutual Insurance, Principal Financial Group, Wells Fargo Bank, Baptist Health Care, BlueCross BlueShield, Carlsberg Beer, Wausau Insurance, Northwestern Mutual, MetLife, The Sports Authority, GlaxoSmithKline, AC Neilsen, IBM, *The New York Post*, and hundreds of others.

## Buy Gitomer, Inc.
**310 Arlington Avenue Loft 329 • Charlotte, North Carolina 28203**
*office* **704/333-1112** • *fax* **704/333-1011**
*e-mail* **jeffrey@gitomer.com** • *web* **www.gitomer.com**

# Acknowledgments and Thanks

**TO JESSICA MCDOUGALL.** My editor, my Jiminy Cricket, my traveling companion, my secret weapon, and my best friend. You are not just the spark. You are the fire. And I respect you and I thank you.

**TO JOSH GITOMER.** For another masterful and tasteful cover design. And for the grounding, real-world, honest, and helpful feedback you provide – whether I ask for it or not.

**TO THE ORIGINAL RESEARCH AND EDITING TEAM OF RACHEL RUSSOTTO, AMANDA DESROCHERS, AND LAURA MILLER.** They have all gone on to greater careers but are still remembered and respected.

**TO GREG RUSSELL.** For a 15-year friendship and a great job of typesetting the original Patterson Principles manuscript. It embraced the content and made the words jump off the pages into your eyes.

**TO MIKE WOLFF.** For re-doing Greg's initial work and transforming it into my "little book" format. Another great job. Not just your design, but also your dedication to the project. It is appreciated beyond words on the page.

**TO MITCHELL KEARNEY, A WORLD-CLASS PHOTOGRAPHER.** Thank you for capturing my image in spite of my hair.

**TO THE NCR SENIOR MANAGEMENT TEAM.** Thank you for being my customer and for supporting this project. And thank you for standing on tradition and continuing to believe in and implement John Patterson's principles.

**TO BARB SWINGER OF NCR.** Thank you for your professionalism, your patience, your input, and your corporate insight. You are not only a pro, you are cool.

**TO THE MONTGOMERY COUNTY HISTORICAL SOCIETY.** Thank you for access to your extensive archives, and thank you for your cooperation.

**TO TIM MOORE AND AMY NEIDLINGER.** I issue a huge thank you for your support, your ideas, and your wisdom. While I don't always accept your offerings, I always respect and appreciate them.

**AND A PERSONAL THANKS TO ALL MY CUSTOMERS AND PROBABLE PURCHASERS.** I appreciate your support and the nice letters and emails you send. I appreciate your business, I appreciate your loyalty, and I appreciate you.

## RESEARCH MATERIAL USED TO FIND AND CORROBORATE FACTS AND PHILOSOPHIES:

*Builders in New Fields*, Charlotte Reeve Conover, 1939.

*He Who Thinks He Can*, Orison Swett Marden, 1908.

*John H. Patterson, Pioneer in Industrial Welfare*, Samuel Crowther, 1926.

*NCR News*, Various editions, 1922-1927.

*Selling Suggestions: Book Two, Efficiency in the Business*, Frank Farrington, 1913.

*The Primer*, Various editions, 1889-1923.

*The Sales Strategy of John H. Patterson*, Roy W. Johnson and Russell W. Lynch, 1932.

# Want the Cha-Ching! Principles for your company?

# Want to become a certified Cha-Ching! Principles presenter?

# Want to add the Cha-Ching! Principles to your training business?

We have developed a complete Cha-Ching! Principles training program that features Jeffrey Gitomer's live seminar (available online or CD-ROM) and a classroom learning package customized for business – and customized just for sales, that assures lesson transferability to your business.

Call 704-333-1112 or e-mail cha-ching@gitomer.com.

# Other titles by Jeffrey Gitomer

### THE LITTLE GREEN BOOK OF GETTING YOUR WAY
(FT Press, 2007)

### THE LITTLE GOLD BOOK OF YES! ATTITUDE
(FT Press, 2007)

### THE LITTLE BLACK BOOK OF CONNECTIONS
(Bard Press, 2006)

### THE LITTLE RED BOOK OF SALES ANSWERS
(FT Press, 2006)

### THE LITTLE RED BOOK OF SELLING
(Bard Press, 2004)

### CUSTOMER SATISFACTION IS WORTHLESS, CUSTOMER LOYALTY IS PRICELESS
(Bard Press, 1998)

### THE SALES BIBLE
(HarperCollins, 1994)